LIGHTHOUSES

NORTON / LIBRARY OF CONGRESS VISUAL SOURCEBOOKS IN ARCHITECTURE, DESIGN, AND ENGINEERING

SARA E. WERMIEL

W. W. Norton & Company, New York and London | In association with the Library of Congress

LIGHTHOUSES

TO MY PARENTS

Library of Congress Cataloging-in-Publication Data

Wermiel, Sara E.
Lighthouses / Sara E. Wermiel.
p. cm. – (Norton/Library of Congress visual
sourcebooks in architecture, design, and engineering)
Includes bibliographical references and index.
ISBN 13: 978-0-393-73166-8
ISBN 10: 0-393-73166-9
1. Lighthouses — United States — Design and
construction — History. 2. Lighthouses — Design
and construction — History. I. Title. II. Series.

TC375.W525 2006
627'.9220973 — dc22   2005058965

ISBN 13: 978-0-393-73166-8
ISBN 10: 0-393-73166-9

W. W. Norton & Company, Inc.,
500 Fifth Avenue, New York, N.Y. 10110
www.wwnorton.com
W. W. Norton & Company Ltd., Castle House,
75/76 Wells St., London W1T 3QT
1 2 3 4 5 6 7 8 9 0

The Center for Architecture, Design and Engineering and the Publishing Office of the Library of Congress are pleased to join with W. W. Norton & Company to publish the pioneering series of the Norton/Library of Congress Visual Sourcebooks in Architecture, Design and Engineering.

Based on the unparalleled collections of the Library of Congress, this series of handsomely illustrated books draws from the collections of the nation's oldest federal cultural institution and the largest library in the world, with more than 130 million items on approximately 530 miles of bookshelves. The collections include more than 19 million books, 2.7 million recordings, 12 million photographs, 4.8 million maps, and 58 million manuscripts.

The subjects of architecture, design, and engineering are threaded throughout the rich fabric of this vast archive, and the books in this new series will serve not only to introduce researchers to the illustrations selected by their authors, but also to build pathways to adjacent and related materials, and even entire archives—to millions of photographs, drawings, prints, views, maps, rare publications, and written information in the general and special collections of the Library of Congress, much of it unavailable elsewhere.

Each volume serves as an entry to the collections, providing a treasury of select visual material, much of it in the public domain, for students, scholars, teachers, researchers, historians of art, architecture, design, technology, and practicing architects, engineers, and designers of all kinds.

A CD-ROM accompanying each volume contains high-quality, downloadable versions of all the illustrations. It offers a direct link to the Library's online, searchable catalogs and image files, including the hundreds of thousands of high-resolution photographs, measured drawings, and data files in the Historic American Buildings Survey, Historic American Engineering Record, and, eventually, the recently inaugurated Historic American Landscape Survey. The Library's Web site has rapidly become one of the most popular and valuable locations on the Internet, experiencing over 3.7 billion hits a year and serving audiences ranging from school children to the most advanced scholars throughout the world, with a potential usefulness that has only begun to be explored.

Among the subjects to be covered in this series are building types, building materials and details; historical periods and movements; landscape architecture and garden design; interior and ornamental design and furnishings; and industrial design. *Lighthouses* is an excellent exemplar of the goals and possibilities on which its series is based.

JAMES H. BILLINGTON
THE LIBRARIAN OF CONGRESS

The introduction to this book provides an overview of the history and development of lighthouses in the United States. It is a view that is broad and inspired by the depth and quality of the resources of the Library of Congress. The balance of the book, containing 476 images, which can be found on the CD at the back of the book, is organized into seven sections, with a special appendix showcasing lighthouses in various artistic mediums. Figure-number prefixes designate the section; the abbreviation "AP" designates the appendix.

Captions give the essential identifying information, where known: subject, location, creator(s) of the image, date, and Library of Congress call number, which can be used to find the image online. Note that a link to the Library of Congress Web site may be found on the CD.

AM	American Memory
AP	Associated Press
DPCC	Detroit Publishing Company Collection
FBJC	Frances Benjamin Johnston Collection
Gen. Coll.	General Collection
G&M	Geography and Map Division
HABS	Historic American Building Survey
HAER	Historic American Engineering Record
LC	Library of Congress
NYWTS	New York World Telegram & Sun Newspaper Photograph Collection
P&P	Prints and Photographs Division
S	Stereograph File
SSF	Subject Specfic File
WC	Wittemann Collection
WTCPC	World's Transportation Commission Photograph Collection

CONTENTS

BUILDING AMERICA'S LIGHTHOUSES

Steadfast, serene, immovable, the same,
Year after year, through all the silent night
Burns on forevermore that quenchless flame,
Shines on that inextinguishable light!
—"The Lighthouse,"
HENRY WADSWORTH LONGFELLOW

Images of lighthouses are among the most beloved iconography in America. Because they inspire positive reactions, lighthouse images have been used to convey steadfastness and strength. They appear on everything from business logos to town seals (IN-001), and their simple shapes and picturesque settings make them enduringly popular subjects for landscape painters and photographers (see Appendix). The form of lighthouse most commonly represented in such images is that of a free-standing, conical tower. While this is a traditional and widespread form, it is but one of a great variety of forms and types of lighthouse structures built in the United States. This variety reflects their different purposes and settings, as well as developments in construction technology.

The focus of this book is the variety of American lighthouse structures. It covers their different forms and materials, as well as some of their designers. Lighthouses are classified by construction type—a function of building materials and form. Each section treats a different type, and an additional section deals with marine foundations. The sections, and structures within the sections, are arranged roughly chronologically. The first two sections deal with masonry towers: the earliest American lighthouses were masonry (stone or brick), and more lighthouses were built of masonry than of any other material. Section Three treats another early type of lighthouse: the cottage-style, in which the tower was built within or attached to the keeper's dwelling. Sections Four and Five treat iron lighthouses: cast-iron plate and skeleton towers. Section Six presents lighthouses on marine foundations—platforms on low-lying or water-covered sites that elevate the lighthouse above the water. The final section treats various construction types introduced in the twentieth century. Missing is a section on freestanding wooden towers. Although many early lighthouses were of this type, and some still stand today, there are

IN-001

IN-001. The Duxbury, Massachusetts, town seal features Duxbury (left) and Gurnet Point (right, twin) lighthouses.

IN-002. Steam fog signal Syren. American Photo-Relief Printing Co., 1873. Gen. Coll., *Annual Report of the Light-House Board*, 1873.

IN-002

too few images of them available to devote a separate section to this construction type. Some of them are illustrated in this introduction (IN-046–IN-055), and wooden towers integrated with dwellings are treated in the section on cottage-style lighthouses (see 3-010–3-012).

PURPOSES AND FORMS OF LIGHTHOUSES

The modern lighthouse — essentially a tower supporting a light that can be seen from a distance, intended to orient mariners and warn them of hazards — came into being in the seventeenth century. Before the era of automation, lamps and other apparatus had to be operated and maintained by keepers, so lighthouses usually had quarters inside or nearby where the keepers, and in many cases their families, lived. In addition to the dwelling, other buildings and equipment at lighthouse sites supported the lights and the keepers — for example, oil houses for storing a supply of lamp fuel, boat sheds, barns, cisterns, boom-derricks, and tramways. Some sites were equipped with fog signals — horns, bells or other noisemakers — used to alert mariners when heavy weather obscured the light (IN-002). Because the lighthouse sites usually included structures in addition to a tower, they came to be called light stations, a more encompassing term befitting the complex of buildings and facilities needed to support the lighthouses' operation.

To understand why lighthouses were built when and where they were, and why they take so many different forms, we should consider why lighthouses were built at all. Lighthouses are called aids to navigation; indeed, before the time of electronic nautical navigation equipment, they were the principal means by which mariners oriented themselves at night or in heavy weather and safely navigated near shore. While landlubbers might imagine that sailors would feel only relief at the sight of land after a long voyage, mariners of the past had reason to fear the coasts, which presented all sorts of hazards. The instruments that in the early nineteenth century enabled a ship to safely cross the trackless oceans could not help it navigate around the shoals and submerged rocks waiting to wreck it just as it neared its port. Markers of all sorts helped mariners get their bearings, but only lighthouses allowed a ship to travel at night and find its way in a storm to safe anchorage.

Commerce was a leading reason for building lighthouses. The lighthouses of the ancient world guided vessels to the ports of important cities. After the Middle Ages, when international trade increased through maritime commerce, the modern lighthouse era began. Merchants seeking to protect their ships and cargos were the main proponents for building lighthouses, and countries with enterprising and progressive merchants and busy ports began to put up lights. In the seventeenth century, Great Britain, then the world's commercial powerhouse, put up the first towers that we would readily recognize as lighthouses. But the residents of North America were not far behind. In the early eighteenth century, as trade between Britain and North America increased, several provincial governments put up lighthouses, making these among the earliest ones of the modern era anywhere. In 1716, when Massachusetts built the first North American lighthouse (Boston Light, on an island in Boston Harbor; IN-042), Great Britain had just eight lighthouses. In the nineteenth century, a time of industrialization and growing worldwide trade, lighthouse construction flowered. At mid-century, the nations with both developed economies and many miles of coastline had the most lighthouses: Great Britain, France, Canada, and the United States. The United States had more lighthouses than any other country.

Lighthouses can be classified according to their purposes. The brightest of the lights were called land-fall, primary coast, or seacoast lights; these were the first ones a ship nearing the coast would see. They might mark the entrance to a river or bay leading to a harbor, or light up the dark parts of the coast between harbors. Harbor lights and secondary lights were not as bright. These dotted the shores of bays and rivers leading to ports and stood at the ends of long piers and breakwaters to help ships avoid running

IN-003

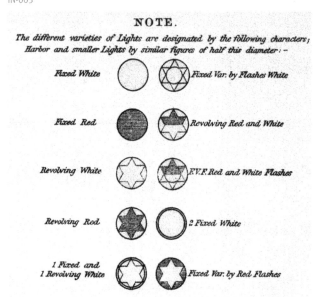

NOTE.

The different varieties of Lights are designated by the following characters;
Harbor and smaller Lights by similar figures of half this diameter:—

Fixed White
Fixed Var. by Flashes White

Fixed Red
Revolving Red and White

Revolving White
F.V.F. Red and White Flashes

Revolving Red
2 Fixed White

1 Fixed and
1 Revolving White
Fixed Var. by Red Flashes

The figures 1, 2, &c., in or near the circles, indicate the orders of the lenses.

IN-004

into them. Lights of various sizes were placed on marine hazards, such as rocks and shoals, to warn ships away. Paired range lights helped mariners navigate narrow channels in rivers and bays: two lights, a low one at the shore and a taller one inland, were situated so that when mariners saw one aligned over the other, they knew their position relative to the channel. The Delaware River leading up to Philadelphia, for example, had many range lights.

The range, or visibility, of a light—the distance at sea from which it can be seen—is a function of the light's brightness and its height above sea level, which is called its focal plane. Seacoast lights, which the U.S. lighthouse administration in the second half of the nineteenth century intended to be visible from 20 to 25 miles away, had to be elevated sufficiently to compensate for the curvature of the earth. This could be accomplished either by putting a light at the top of a tall tower or by building a lighthouse on a hill or promontory. An example of the latter is the small tower at Point Reyes, California (IN-003); because it is on a steep bluff, it has a focal plane of 294 feet. Sometimes lights were placed too high and therefore were not visible near shore. Thus, some on California's mountainous coast had to be relocated from their high original positions to lower sites.

It was very important that each light be distinguishable from surrounding lights so that mariners could determine their true location. Many wrecks occurred when shipmasters mistook one light for another. Thus, each lighthouse in a region was assigned a unique visual pattern, called the character of the light. Lights revolved, flashed, or were fixed; they showed different colors (red, blue, and green); and they were grouped— paired horizontally in adjacent towers (called twin lights) or vertically in one tower, or even, in one case, arranged in a cluster of three. Features could be combined (for example, color and flashing) to create a distinctive character. When there was no danger of

IN-003. Point Reyes Lighthouse soon after completion, looking west toward the Pacific Ocean, Point Reyes, California. Eadweard Muybridge, photographer, ca. 1871. P&P, S, lot 13506.

IN-004. "U.S. Light-House Establishment, Chart Showing the Relative Positions of Lights in the Seventh Light-House District." 1872. G&M, U.S., Light Houses, 7th District, U.S. Light-House Board.

Detail of map showing the key symbols for different characters of lights.

IN-005

IN-005. Old Harbor Beacon, Savannah, Georgia. Branan Sanders, photographer, 1934. P&P, HABS, GA,26-SAV,23-1.

This illuminated harbor beacon, erected in 1868, guided mariners navigating the Savannah River.

IN-006. Cleveland Lighthouse, Cleveland, Ohio. Aubert Père (after Bodmer), illustrator, 1840–1843. P&P, LC-USZ62-70559.

Although labeled as a lighthouse, this presumably is a picture of the illuminated beacon on a pier in Cleveland Harbor, established in 1831.

IN-006

mistaking one light for another, characters could be repeated. After the Civil War, the U.S. Light-House Board—the office that administered the nation's lighthouse service during the second half of the nineteenth century—issued maps that showed the location, type, and range of lights along the nation's coasts and shores (IN-004).

Lighthouses were not the only sorts of illuminated aids to navigation found in the nineteenth century. Beacon-lights or tide-lights were fixed, lighted structures with a small range (IN-005–IN-006). Lighthouse keepers often maintained them in addition to their regular lighthouse lamps. Light-boats or light-vessels, later called lightships, served as floating lighthouses. First used in England in the eighteenth century, they were introduced in the United States in 1820, when one was stationed in the Chesapeake Bay. Lightships were usually moored at dangerous offshore places such as sandbars and shoals, where lighthouses could not be built economically. Because of the limited height at which a light could be placed on these boats, and the high cost of maintaining them, they were replaced with lighthouses when funds and new technology permitted. Nevertheless, lightships were an important component of the nation's navigational aids, and their use continued at some locations well into the twentieth century (IN-007–IN-010).

Aids to navigation included nonilluminated structures and devices, too, such as monuments, spindles (poles), trivets (three-legged stands), and unlighted beacons, usually fixed to rocks; and floating buoys and dolphins (mooring buoys). Nonilluminated structures that could be seen from a distance were called daymarks or day-beacons. Lighthouses also could serve as daymarks, which is why they were sometimes painted in bright colors or with bold patterns (example, stripes or diamonds) (IN-011).

Compared with Americans in the nineteenth century, people today have relatively

IN-007

IN-008

IN-009

IN-007. Five Fathom Bank light-vessel, New Jersey. N. L. Stebbins, photographer, ca. 1891. P&P, LC-USZ62-121578.

IN-008. Fenwick Island Shoal light-vessel, Delaware. N. L. Stebbins, photographer, ca. 1891. P&P, LC-USZ62-121579.

IN-009. Boston lightship, Massachusetts. Unidentified photographer, ca. 1906. DPCC, LC-USZ62-71894.

opposite
IN-010. Sandy Hook lightship, New Jersey. Charles E. Bolles, photographer, ca. 1900. P&P, LC-USZ62-71304.

IN-011. Day-beacon on Seaflower Reef, Long Island Sound, New York. American Photo-Relief Printing Co., Philadelphia, 1873. Gen. Coll., *Annual Report of the Light-House Board*, 1873.

IN-012. "The River Swarming with Craft." Gen. Coll., *Harper's New Monthly Magazine* 43 (September 1871): 482.

IN-010

IN-011

IN-012

little experience with ship travel or maritime commerce. But from the eighteenth century through the first part of the twentieth century, coinciding with the period of lighthouse construction, water transport was for a time the main—and later, along with railroads, the most important—means of long-distance transport for both people and goods. Ports swarmed with vessels of all types, from small ferries and boats plying the coasts and rivers to large ocean-going and military ships. Cars, buses, trains, and airplanes have largely superseded ferries and ocean-liners for transporting people. Technological innovations have greatly reduced the ranks of longshoremen. The once bustling docks in many port towns are now long gone. Historic images suggest how active ports once were and, consequently, the importance of lighthouses at this time (IN-012–IN-023).

It is also hard for people today to imagine the difficulties mariners faced piloting the coasts at a time when only light stations could reveal the entrance to a harbor at night or in a storm. Reading contemporary sailing directions, such as those in *The American Coast Pilot*, the leading guide in the first half of the nineteenth century, gives a sense of how mariners used lights and daymarks to shape a course. Here, for example, are directions for sailing up the Delaware River, heading for Wilmington or Philadelphia, from the eleventh edition (1827):

IN-013

IN-014

16 BUILDING AMERICA'S LIGHTHOUSES

IN-013. Riverfront, Jacksonville, Florida. Unidentified photographer, ca. 1904. DPCC, P&P, LC-D4-17505.

IN-014. Harbor, New Bedford, Massachusetts. Lemuel D. Eldred, artist, 1903. P&P, LC-USZ62-126591.

IN-015. Harbor, Gulfport, Mississippi. Unidentified photographer, ca. 1906. DPCC, LC-D4-15500 L.

IN-016. Harbor, Gulfport, Mississippi. Unidentified photographer, ca. 1906. DPCC, LC-D4-15500 L.

IN-017. Harbor, Gulfport, Mississippi. Unidentified photographer, ca. 1906. DPCC, LC-D4-15500 L.

IN-018. Harbor, Gulfport, Mississippi. Unidentified photographer, ca. 1906. DPCC, LC-D4-15500 L.

IN-019. Harbor, Gulfport, Mississippi. Unidentified photographer, ca. 1906. DPCC, LC-D4-15500 L.

IN-015

IN-016

IN-017

IN-018

IN-019

IN-020

IN-021

IN-022

IN-020. Sacramento and Oakland steamers in the harbor of San Francisco, California. Lawrence & Houseworth, publisher. Unidentified photographer, 1866. P&P, LC-USZ62-27491.

IN-021. Chicago River east from Rush Street Bridge, Chicago, Illinois. Unidentified photographer, ca. 1905. DPCC, P&P, LC-D4-18839.

IN-022. Harbor and waterfront, Boston, Massachusetts. Unidentified photographer, ca. 1906. DPCC, LC-USZ62-77183.

IN-023. Harbor entrance and lighthouse, Charlevoix, Michigan. Unidentified photographer, ca. 1900. DPCC, LC-D4-12293 A.

IN-023

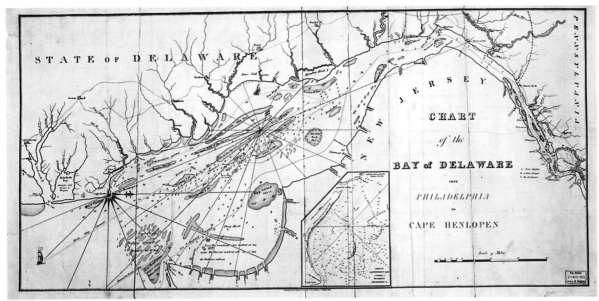

IN-024

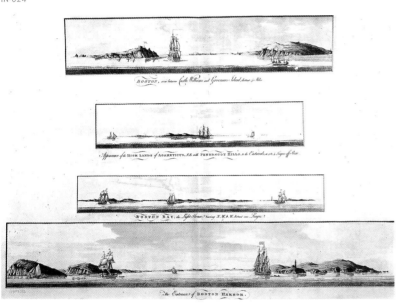

IN-025

IN-024. Chart of the Bay of Delaware from Philadelphia to Cape Henlopen. 1823. G&M, U.S., Delaware Bay.

Detail of an 1823 chart showing the features described in the excerpt from *The American Coast Pilot*. The lighthouse on Brandywine Shoal had not yet been built.

IN-025. Eighteenth-century view showing landmarks on the New England coast and at the entrance to Boston Harbor, including the first Boston Light. Joseph F. W. Des Barres, engraver, 1777. P&P, LC-USZ62-46056.

"In running up the Bay, keep the old light-house [Cape Henlopen Lighthouse] to bear S. 1/2 E. until you pass the *Beacon Boat* with one mast, on the Brown, distant 12 miles, then steer N. by W. for the light-house on the Brandywine Shoal until you are within half a mile, then steer N. N. W. for the upper part of the Brandywine, on which there is a *Beacon Boat* with two masts; then steer N. W. by N. for the lower part of the Fourteen Feet Bank, on which there is a small Buoy"[1] (IN-024–IN-025). By the second half of the nineteenth century, scientific surveys of the coasts began to become available, which greatly aided mariners navigating the coasts.

[1] *American Coast Pilot*, 1827.

HISTORY OF THE U.S. LIGHTHOUSE SYSTEM

Eleven lighthouses, built by several colonial governments, are known to have existed in North America before the Revolutionary War. The Province of Massachusetts erected the first of these in 1716 on Beacon (also known as Little Brewster) Island to signal the entrance to Boston Harbor leading to the port of Boston, the busiest and most prosperous port in eighteenth-century America. This masonry tower stood about 65 feet tall. The other ten were built between the 1740s and the 1770s. Two were located in the South (at Tybee Island, marking the way to Savannah, Georgia, and at the harbor in Charleston, South Carolina), while two more (Brant Point on Nantucket Island and Gurnet Point in Plymouth) were in Massachusetts. The early lighthouses were masonry or wood.

Following the Revolutionary War, one of the first acts of the new federal government was to make lighthouse construction and maintenance a national, rather than state, responsibility. The cost of the service was to be paid for out of the treasury of the United States rather than through fees charged to passing vessels, as had been done in the colonial period (and which continued to be the way Great Britain financed its coastal lights in the nineteenth century). The U.S. government, from the beginning, recognized that the safeguarding of lives and property at sea was a national trust and duty. The first lighthouse bill, enacted in 1789, provided for the construction of a lighthouse at the entrance of the Chesapeake Bay, and a site at Cape Henry on the Virginia side was chosen. Lighted in 1792, Cape Henry Lighthouse is notable as the nation's first federal public work. Management of the lighthouse system was assigned to the Secretary of the Treasury because he headed the department that collected duties on foreign trade, and lighthouses were considered aids to commerce (IN-026; see also 1-009–1-010).

In 1800, after adding a few new lighthouses and taking control of state lighthouses, the United States operated a total of sixteen lighthouses. Over the next twenty years, the nation added thirty-nine more, for a total of fifty-five. During this time, central supervision of the lighthouse system bounced around the executive branch of government.

IN-026. Original logo of the Public Works Historical Society depicting the nation's first federal public work, Old Cape Henry Lighthouse (see also 1-009–1-010).

Then, in 1820, overall responsibility was placed in the office of the Fifth Auditor of the U.S. Treasury, where it remained for the next thirty-two years. During this entire time, Stephen Pleasonton held the position of Fifth Auditor.

Along with the nation's population, land area, and maritime commerce, the number of lighthouses increased steadily during the first half of the nineteenth century, but the process for getting them built left much to be desired. At this time, Congress determined key matters relating to lighthouses: where they would be built and, since Congress appropriated specific sums for individual structures, what they would be like. Lighthouses went up at places where constituents demanded them. This resulted in too many lighthouses in some places and too few where they were more urgently needed but population was sparse. Before 1837, no proposed site was examined objectively to ascertain the necessity for a lighthouse there. Then, in the lighthouse appropriations act of that year, Congress for the first time ordered a Board of Navy Commissioners to evaluate and make recommendations about sites. The Board's report led to the suspension of plans for thirty-one proposed lighthouses. After this, Congress and the Fifth Auditor sought reports from qualified, independent inspectors about potential sites. Although this process helped the government determine the need for any given proposed lighthouse, there was still was no system for judging the importance of one site compared to others, so as to prioritize construction.

Moreover, the process for building the lighthouses resulted in many buildings of poor quality. The amounts Congress appropriated for construction were rarely based on detailed estimates of the cost of building a structure at a particular site. During Pleasonton's administration, plans generally came from the Treasury Department and the buildings were constructed by contract in accordance with federal bidding laws, which required public advertisement and the awarding of contracts to the lowest bidder. Collectors of customs at the ports served as superintendents of the lighthouses in their districts, and they were responsible for choosing the exact place where a new lighthouse would stand. They also accepted the finished building so the contractor could be paid.

Collectors got their jobs through political connections rather than on the basis of their engineering and maritime expertise, and they generally did not give lighthouses the attention the structures needed. The main advantage of this process was its low cost, since the process made use of officials already on the government payroll. However, neither the collectors nor the Fifth Auditor were qualified to select the best sites or structural designs.

At the end of the 1830s, Congress and the Secretary of the Treasury received many complaints about the lighthouse service as well as recommendations for improving it. Some people criticized the visibility of the lights and the lack of procedures for notifying the maritime community when new lights were established or a light's character was changed. While Pleasonton defended the service's management, arguing that the system was cost-effective and self-policing, the critics charged otherwise, asserting that overall America's lighthouses were inferior to those of Great Britain and France. Essentially, the critics were demanding that more staff—and qualified staff—be devoted to the cause of lighting the coasts.

Indeed, the problems with the lighthouse service stemmed from Congress trying to build and maintain a large lighthouse system on the cheap. Between 1820, when Pleasonton took charge of the lighthouse service, and 1837, the number of lighthouses increased from 55 with no light-vessels to 208 lighthouses and 26 light-vessels. Yet Pleasonton's request to hire two additional clerks to handle the growing workload went unheeded by Congress. Even after Pleasonton got additional clerks, his staff remained miniscule. In 1842, when the lighthouse system included 256 lighthouses, 30 light-vessels, and many beacons, buoys, and other aids to navigation, only four clerks worked on lighthouse business. Moreover, the sums Congress appropriated for particular structures were often unrealistically low. In such cases, Pleasonton sometimes put off constructing a lighthouse and applied for additional funds; at other times, he proceeded with a project and ended up with an inadequate structure. The naval officers who inspected lighthouses in 1838 on orders from Congress discovered many poorly constructed towers.

Some contemporary and all modern writers blame Pleasonton for these failures, dismissing him as incompetent or at least penny-pinching. But while Pleasonton may have been overly scrupulous about spending public money, there are many indications that he wanted better buildings and would have built them if bidding regulations and lack of funds had not tied his hands. For example, he tried to assign the more technically challenging lighthouse structures to qualified engineers. In 1847, referring to the lighthouse authorized for a difficult site in Long Island Sound, Execution Rocks (see 1-093–1-095), he wrote, "In cases like this requiring science to plan and execute the work I am in favor of employing persons thus qualified, as I am sure Mr. [Gridley] Bryant is, without running the hazard of having the work half done by ignorant persons who may be the lowest bidders, under an advertizement for proposals."[2] And indeed, for this project he was able to hire an experienced engineer, Alexander Parris. When Congress appropriated $20,000 to build a seawall to protect the deteriorating Whale's Back Lighthouse at Portsmouth, New Hampshire, Pleasonton urged that the lighthouse be replaced with a new, more durable structure, even though doing so would cost an estimated $75,000. But Congress did not accept his suggestion.

Harsh conditions and neglect also shortened the lifespan and diminished the effectiveness of lighthouses. Even well-built structures fell into ruin when their foundations were undermined, eroded away, or became submerged. Moreover, the energy and reliability of keepers in maintaining the lights and other structures affected the quality of the lights and the condition of the stations. In Pleasonton's time, keepers were political appointees, underpaid and not subject to regular supervision. A light's poor performance might be as much the result of the keeper's neglect as of deficiencies in the design of the apparatus or tower.

Given the situation of the lighthouse administration in the Treasury Department, Pleasonton did not have the resources the system required, nor could he enlist other

---

[2] Stephen Pleasonton to Alexander Parris, letter dated 21 April 1847. Alexander Parris Papers, Massachusetts State House Library. Punctuation added.

officials to help him in an ongoing way without committing bureaucratic suicide. Reorganization occurred in 1852, when management of the system was transferred to a Light-House Board.

This transfer followed a comprehensive survey undertaken by a joint public and private board authorized by Congress in 1851. Congress ordered the Treasury Department to convene a special board dominated by military personnel to examine the lighthouse service and recommend a program for improvement. Reporting in 1852, the Light-House Board concluded that only a new management structure could overcome the deficiencies of the current system. Congress then made the Light-House Board permanent and gave it responsibility for overall administration of the lighthouse service. While the Board technically was still attached to the Treasury Department, with the Secretary of the Treasury as its President, it acted largely independently. Moreover, with six of the nine board members representing the U.S. Army and Navy, it had a military orientation. In this respect, the reorganized lighthouse administration emulated the lighthouse service in France, considered the world's finest, which was supervised by engineers of the quasi-military government engineering service, the Corps des Ponts et Chaussées (corps of bridges and roads). The Light-House Board remained in charge of the U.S. lighthouse system until 1910.

During this time, U.S. Army engineers had responsibility for lighthouse design, construction, renovation, and repair. Congress continued to authorize funds for individual lighthouses; however, the Light-House Board was more involved in reviewing requests for new lights and making recommendations. The Board divided the coasts into districts—twelve, initially—and assigned an engineer officer to each. Each district also had an inspector who helped to supply the lights and the keepers, although sometimes the district engineer served in both capacities. All of the district engineers, along with the Board's engineer secretary—its executive officer for construction and maintenance— were officers in the U.S. Army Corps of Engineers or Corps of Topographical Engineers (until the latter corps was merged with the Corps of Engineers during the Civil War).

IN-027. Index map, "United States Light-House Establishment, Outline Map Showing Districts and a Few Important Lights." 1896. G&M, U.S., Light Houses, U.S. Light-House Board.

IN-027

The Light-House Board approved sites and had final say over the designs for light-houses. The district engineers often proposed designs for new lighthouses; they also proposed renovations to existing ones. Once a design was approved, the district engineer oversaw construction.

With their engineering orientation, the district engineers and engineer officers of the Light-House Board adopted and adapted new technology for building lighthouses. They followed British and Continental lighthouse developments and borrowed ideas for the American service. The engineer officers, who trained at the U.S. Military Academy at West Point, were assisted by civil engineers and draftsmen employed by the Light-House Board. Also contributing to the design of lighthouses were the contractors who actually built the structures. Despite a military inclination toward standardization, light-houses were and are quite varied in design and materials.

The Board had a comprehensive vision for lighting the coasts and, with officers stationed in all the districts, was able to obtain current information on which to base its decisions. Over time, the territory encompassed by the United States increased and maritime business expanded in formerly little-traveled areas—all of which created the demand for more lighthouses. The number of lighthouse districts increased to sixteen in 1886, and then to nineteen in the twentieth century. Given the vast extent of coasts and shores to light, the United States had more lighthouses than any other nation (IN-027–IN-030).

The building of lighthouses at remote and technically challenging places, notably the offshore rocks and shoals, was arduous and perilous. Construction usually took several years. Workmen lived at the sites during the building seasons, on ships or sometimes in

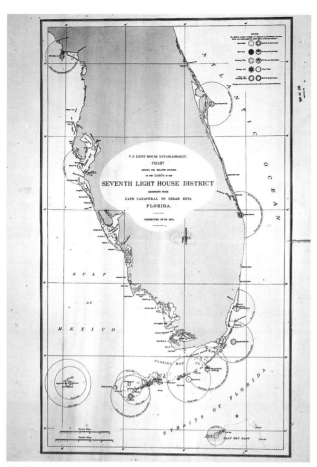

IN-028

IN-028. Detail of map showing the Straits of Florida, "U.S. Light-House Establishment, Chart Showing the Relative Positions of Lights in the Seventh Light-House District." 1872. G&M, U.S., Light Houses, 7th District, U.S. Light-House Board.

IN-029. Detail of map showing the Great Lakes region, "U.S. Light-House Establishment, Chart Showing the Relative Positions of the Lights in the Eleventh Light-House District." 1875–1876. G&M, U.S., Light Houses, U.S. Light-House Establishment, District 11.

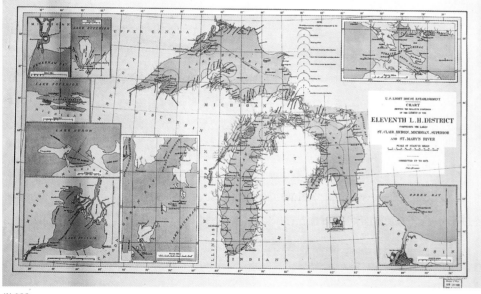

IN-029

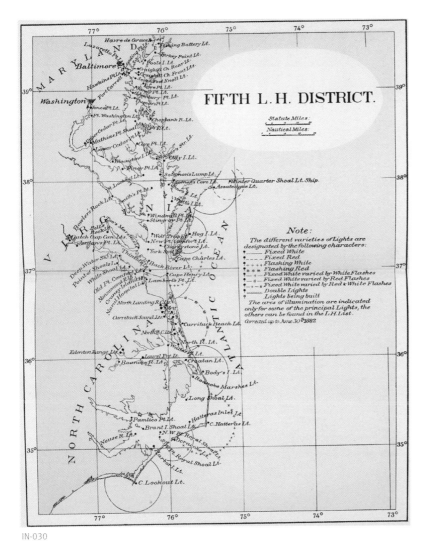

IN-030

IN-030. Map showing locations and ranges of lighthouses, Fifth Light-House District. 1882. Gen. Coll., *Annual Report of the Light-House Board*, 1882.

barracks far from shore that were put up on the sites where lighthouses were being built. These tradesmen—masons, carpenters, ironworkers—labored in cold and wet conditions; some lost their lives when waves swept them and their equipment from the worksites. Although the heroism of lighthouse keepers of the past is celebrated, the bravery, skill, and ingenuity of these tradesmen are essentially unknown and unsung. Their accomplishments must speak for them: some of the most important engineering landmarks in America are the offshore lighthouses.

Early in the twentieth century, the lighthouse service was transferred to the Bureau of Lighthouses in the Department of Commerce and Labor, a move that put it under civilian control. Then, in 1939, the functions of the Bureau, along with hundreds of lighthouses, were transferred to the U.S. Coast Guard. The Coast Guard at the time had little in the way of onshore facilities and engineering expertise, so it established a Civil Engineering Division. It continued a program of replacing the oil lamps still in use with electric lights and also began to automate the lighthouses, a process that accelerated in the 1960s. Today all American lighthouses are automated. The Coast Guard continues to oversee the nation's aids to navigation.

LIGHTHOUSE ILLUMINATION

The first concern of the lighthouse builder is how far from shore a light can be seen by a passing vessel. A light's visibility is a function of its brightness and the height of the tower on which it sits. Seacoast lights, which had to be visible from the greatest distance, contained the brightest lighting apparatus set at a high focal plane—either on high ground or atop a tall tower. Before the 1850s, there was little science in determining what this focal plane should be, and the lighting apparatus in use in the United States at the time was not efficient.

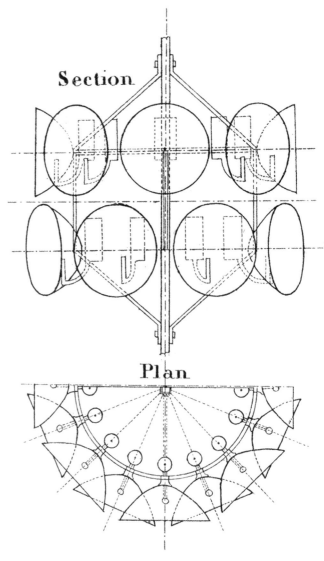

Section

Plan

IN-031

The illuminating apparatus of a lighthouse consists of a source of light (a lamp) and a device for focusing the light and sending it in the direction where it is needed. Lights in the colonial era may have been fueled by coal and candles simply glowing on a tower. Around the turn of the nineteenth century, spider lamps were introduced: consisting of wicks in a pan of oil, these too operated without magnification or focus, and their light dissipated ineffectively in all directions, not only out to sea. Ships had to approach close to the lights to see them. Beginning in 1812, a new system of lighting introduced a more modern lamp and a parabolic reflector. Derived from one invented by the Swiss chemist Aimé Argand, the lamp had a cylindrical wick and received an air supply from a central draft tube, enabling it to burn much more brightly than the spider lamp for the amount of oil consumed. Behind each lamp was a concave, parabolic-shaped reflector coated with silvered metal, designed to turn back and concentrate the light rays to form a beam. Similar lighting systems were used at the time in Great Britain and France. The U.S. government bought the patent for the American version from its inventor, the American ship captain Winslow Lewis, and had his apparatus installed in the nation's forty-nine lighthouses, a task completed in 1815. Some of the lights had a green glass "lens" in front of the lamp as well as a reflector, although this lens proved to be of little value.

Lighthouses received different numbers of lamps with reflectors depending on the required range and character of the light; an important lighthouse might have as many as twenty. While they were better than the common lamps, these catoptric (reflecting) lights had a number of drawbacks — for example, the silvered surface of the reflectors wore off in the course of cleaning, and the lamps consumed great quantities of oil (IN-031–IN-032).

IN-031. Fixed light catoptric (reflecting) apparatus. 1846. Gen. Coll., plate 16, volume of plates accompanying the *Report . . . on improvements in the light-house system . . .*, Senate doc. no. 488, 29:1.

opposite
IN-032. Section and plan of a revolving catoptric (reflecting) light apparatus. 1846. Gen. Coll., plate 16, volume of plates accompanying the *Report . . . on improvements in the light-house system . . .*, Senate doc. no. 488, 29:1.

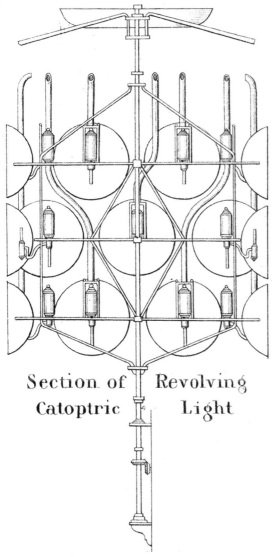

Section of Revolving Catoptric Light

Plan of Revolving Catoptric Light

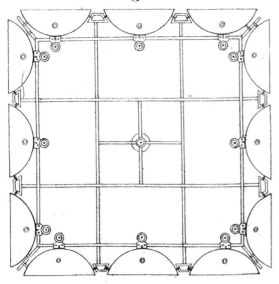

Meanwhile, in France, a new kind of lighthouse-illuminating apparatus had been introduced: a dioptric, or refracting, lens light. Named for its inventor, Augustin Jean Fresnel, a civil engineer and mathematician, the lens operated very differently from the reflector. The lens was made of sections of prismatic glass placed in front of a lamp, most commonly encircling the lamp. Rather than reflecting the light of the lamp, the Fresnel lens redirected it. Above and below the center of the lens, prisms bent the lamp's light toward the middle, where a bulls-eye of glass magnified it. The result was a concentrated, horizontal beam of light. Fresnel introduced his apparatus in French lighthouses beginning in the 1820s. At the time, France's lighthouse system was generally considered the most efficient in the world, with the best lights.

In the 1830s, critics of the American lighthouse service demanded that the United States adopt Fresnel's new illuminating system. As part of an 1838 act making appropriations for building lighthouses and other aids to navigation, Congress ordered the acquisition of two sets of the "lenticular apparatus," the Fresnel lenses, in order to test them against American lights. These were to be made at the workshop of the renowned lensmaker Henry Lapaute in Paris. Although the U.S. government contracted to pay what must have seemed an astronomical sum of $12,607 for the pair, in the end they cost twice this amount, after including the cost of shipping and setting them up with the assistance of a workman from Lapaute's shop. In comparison, the cost of patent lamps and reflectors around this time for new, smaller lighthouses was under $500.

Cost aside, the experiment was a great success. The lenses were put in Navesink Light in 1841; compared to the reflectors, the brightness of the French lens light was indisputably better. Stephen Pleasonton

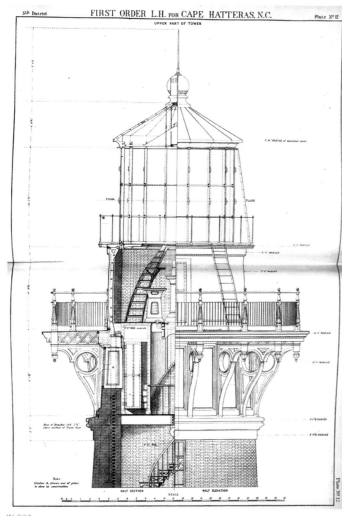

IN-033

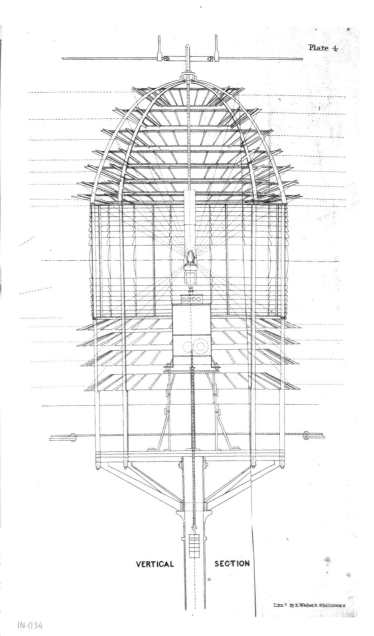

VERTICAL   SECTION

IN-034

praised the beauty and excellence of the lenses and considered them the perfection of apparatus for lighthouse purposes. Yet his enthusiasm for the lens light was tempered by his concern that ordinary lighthouse keepers could not manage them properly. He therefore recommended that these lights be installed only in lighthouses near large towns, where qualified staff and materials to maintain the lights could be more readily obtained. This consideration, the high cost of the apparatus, and the additional cost of modifying existing lighthouse lanterns to accommodate a larger lens slowed the introduction of Fresnel lenses in American lighthouses before the 1850s.

After the Light-House Board took control in the 1850s, it began the process of substituting Fresnel lenses for the old reflectors. The Board concluded that lighthouse keepers, properly instructed, would be able to maintain the valuable lenses. With the new lenses, the Board could better classify lighthouses according to their importance. Formerly, lighthouses had been classified by a rudimentary system according to height; the tallest towers were about 65 feet high and the smallest about 30 feet. Fresnel lenses were classified according to the size, called order, of the lens—specifically, the distance

IN-033. Vertical section (left) and elevation (right) of the top of the tower, Cape Hatteras Lighthouse, north of Cape Hatteras Point/Outer Banks, North Carolina. 1869. Gen. Coll., *Specifications for a Light-House to be Erected at Cape Hatteras, North Carolina* (Washington, DC: G.P.O., 1869).

IN-034. Drawing of a Fresnel lens from an early American report on this apparatus. 1846. Gen. Coll., plate 16, volume of plates accompanying the *Report . . . on improvements in the light-house system . . .*, Senate doc. no. 488, 29:1.

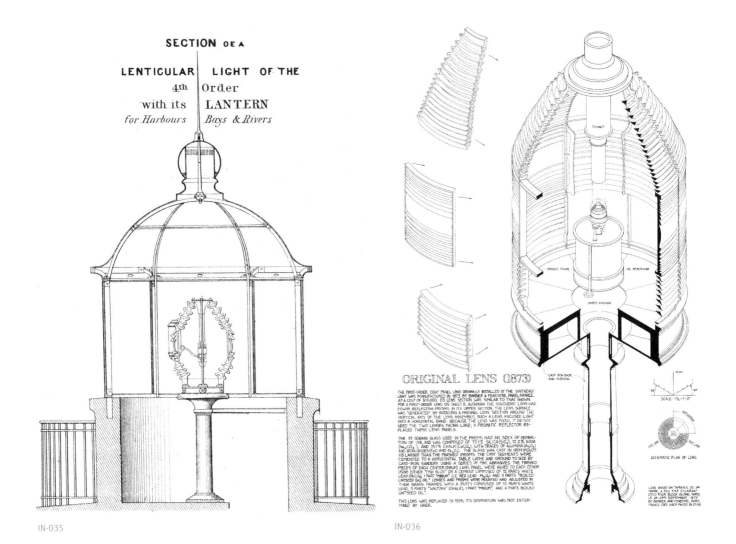

SECTION of a
LENTICULAR LIGHT OF THE
4th Order
with its LANTERN
for Harbours Bays & Rivers

ORIGINAL LENS (1873)

THE FIRST-ORDER, EIGHT PANEL LENS ORIGINALLY INSTALLED AT THE SOUTHEAST
LIGHT WAS MANUFACTURED IN 1873 BY BARBIER & FENESTRE, PARIS, FRANCE,
AT A COST OF $10,000. ITS LENS SECTION WAS SIMILAR TO THAT SHOWN
FOR A FIRST-ORDER LENS ON SHEET 8. ALTHOUGH THE SOUTHEAST LENS HAD
FEWER REFLECTING PRISMS IN ITS UPPER SECTION. THE LENS SURFACE
WAS "GENERATED" BY ROTATING A FRESNEL LENS SECTION AROUND THE
VERTICAL AXIS OF THE LENS ASSEMBLY. SUCH A LENS FOCUSED LIGHT
INTO A HORIZONTAL BAND. BECAUSE THE LENS WAS FIXED, IT DID NOT
NEED THE TWO LENSES FACING LAND, A PRISMATIC REFLECTOR RE-
PLACED THESE LENS PANELS.

THE ST. GOBAIN GLASS USED IN THE PRISMS HAD AN INDEX OF REFRAC-
TION OF 1.54, AND WAS COMPOSED OF 72.1% SILICA(SiO_2), 12.2% SODA
(Na_2CO_3), AND 15.7% CHALK ($CaCO_3$), WITH TRACES OF ALUMINA(Al_2O_3)
AND IRON OXIDES(FeO AND Fe_2O_3). THE GLASS WAS CAST IN IRON MOLDS
1/8 LARGER THAN THE FINISHED PRISMS. THE CAST SEGMENTS WERE
CEMENTED TO A HORIZONTAL TABLE LATHE AND GROUND TO SIZE BY
CAST-IRON SANDERS USING A SERIES OF FINE ABRASIVES. THE FINISHED
PIECES OF EACH CENTER (DRUM) LENS PANEL WERE GLUED TO EACH OTHER
USING EITHER "FISH GLUE" OR A CEMENT COMPOSED OF 12 PARTS WHITE
LEAD (Pb_3O_4), 1 PART "MINIUM" (I.E. RED LEAD Pb_3O_4) AND 5 PARTS "BOILED
LINTSEED [sic] OIL." LENSES AND PRISMS WERE MOUNTED AND ADJUSTED IN
THEIR BRASS FRAMES WITH A PUTTY COMPOSED OF 12 PARTS WHITE
LEAD, 5 PARTS "WHITING" (CHALK), 1 PART "MINIUM", AND 4 PARTS BOILED
LINTSEED OIL.

THIS LENS WAS REPLACED IN 1929. ITS DISPOSITION WAS NOT DETER-
MINED BY HAER.

IN-035   IN-036

IN-035. Drawing of a fourth order Fresnel lens in a lantern. 1846. Gen. Coll., plate 16, volume of plates accompanying the *Report . . . on improvements in the light-house system . . .*, Senate doc. no. 488, 29:1.

IN-036. Drawing of a first order Fresnel lens originally installed in the Block Island Southeast Light Station, Block Island, Rhode Island. Patricio Del Real, delineator, 1988. HAER, RI,5-NESH,1-, sheet no. 9.

As this lens no longer exists, the drawing is based on contemporary documentation and the sole known surviving photograph, which shows a first order fixed white light, installed 1874 and first illuminated February 1, 1875. The lens was removed in 1929.

of the light source from the lens and the number of wicks, and therefore brightness, of the lamp. The largest, first order lenses had the widest diameters and their lamps had four or five wicks. These were placed in the most important seacoast lights, which became first order lights. Second order lights had three wicks. The smallest, sixth order lights, with a small diameter and single wick, were placed in harbor lights. By the end of the 1860s, most of America's five hundred-plus lighthouses had Fresnel lenses, including twenty-six first order, nineteen second order, and sixty-two third order lights. However, parabolic reflector lights continued to have their place: they were used in range lights and on lightships in the second half of the nineteenth century.

The form of lanterns changed over the course of the century, both to improve efficiency and to accommodate the large lenses. Old-style lanterns have been called the birdcage type; surviving examples are rare (see 3-001–3-002). An example of the more modern type is the one on the second Cape Hatteras Lighthouse (1870). It was topped with a ball that served as a ventilator for the smoky lamp (IN-033–IN-041).

Along with replacing reflectors with Fresnel lenses, the Light-House Board began instituting a more comprehensive system of lighting the coasts. It intended to light not

IN-037

IN-038

IN-039

IN-037. Block Island Southeast Light Station, Block Island, Rhode Island. Ca. 1918. Original in collection of Block Island Historical Society. HAER, RI,5-NESH,1-26.

IN-038. Third order Fresnel bivalve lens, installed 1910, in Split Rock Lighthouse, Two Harbors Vic., Minnesota. Jet Lowe, photographer, 1990. P&P, HAER, MINN,38-TWOHA.V,1-4.

View inside the lantern looking up at the Fresnel lens.

IN-039. Closeup of Fresnel lens inside the lighthouse lantern, Split Rock Lighthouse, Two Harbors Vic., Minnesota. Jet Lowe, photographer, 1990. P&P, HAER, MINN, 38-TWOHA.V,1-7.

Figures IN-040 and IN-041 give a sense of the scale of the lenses.

IN-040

IN-040. Fire Island Lighthouse, Fire Island, New York. 1934. P&P, NYWTS, SUBJ/GEOG: LIGHTHOUSES–FIRE ISLAND–N.Y.S.

Assistant Keeper Gus Axelson, standing inside a Fresnel lens, preheats the oil gas vapor light before igniting it.

IN-041. Coney Island Lighthouse, Brooklyn, New York. Roger Higgins, photographer, 1961. NYWTS, SUBJ/GEOG: LIGHTHOUSES–SEAGATE LIGHT–NEW YORK HARBOR.

Keeper Frank Schubert opens the Fresnel lens in order to clean it. Note that this image was incorrectly catalogued as Sea Gate Light.

IN-041

only entrances to rivers and harbors but the entire coastline, so that mariners could always determine their position. Seacoast lights were placed so that ships would never be out of range of one of these primary lights. Between them were secondary lights, which marked hazards or the entries to rivers and harbors. As a result of this policy, the number and variety of lighthouses increased considerably.

LIGHTHOUSE CONSTRUCTION TYPES

In some of our light-house localities, the unbroken force of ocean waves must be resisted; in others, the less powerful waves of bays and harbors only take effect; while in others, the sites are entirely withdrawn from watery inroads. Hence the different constructions demand quite different degrees of skill; but, in all, the faithful builder . . . ought in every instance to insure that the costly teachings of past experience are made duly and appropriately effective.[3]

---

[3] "Light-house Construction and Illumination," *Putnam's Monthly Magazine* 8 (August 1856): 198.

IN-042

Nearly all lighthouses built in America from the colonial period to the mid-nineteenth century were made of masonry—stone and brick—or of wood. While the first Boston Light was a conical tower probably built of brick (IN-042), the most common form of masonry tower in the early days was the octagonal, pyramidal tower with stone walls. This form continued to be constructed through the 1850s. By this time, the use of brick became more widespread. Masonry was used for the longest time, and more lighthouses were built of this material than any other. Although the material is traditional, masonry towers could be a challenge to build, given the often soft and shifting ground at lighthouse sites. The taller towers required well-designed foundations to keep the structures secure and prevent them from overturning in a gale. Thus, lighthouses might be built on piles or grillages, the latter a structure made of horizontal layers of timber, each layer perpendicular to the previous one.

Once the Light-House Board took control of the system and put lighthouse design and construction in the hands of professional engineers, more structurally ambitious masonry towers began to appear. A premier example is America's first sea-rock masonry tower, the second Minot's Ledge Lighthouse near Cohasset, Massachusetts, constructed in the 1850s (IN-043). Also at this time, engineers began to build towers 150 feet tall or higher. To create a sequence of seacoast lights, the Light-House Board designated existing towers as primary lights and selected locations for new ones. The height of many of the existing towers was raised, and new towers were built to unprecedented heights. One of the first towers to reach 150 feet above sea level was the 1803 Cape Hatteras Lighthouse in North Carolina (IN-044), which was raised from 95 feet above

IN-043. Waves crashing against Minot's Ledge Lighthouse, off Cohasset, Massachusetts. P&P, S, lot 13468.

IN-044. Cape Hatteras Lighthouse mirrored in a pool, Cape Hatteras, North Carolina. 1938. ACME, P&P, NYWTS, SUBJ/GEOG: LIGHTHOUSES–CAPE HATTERAS–NORTH CAROLINA.

IN-043

IN-044

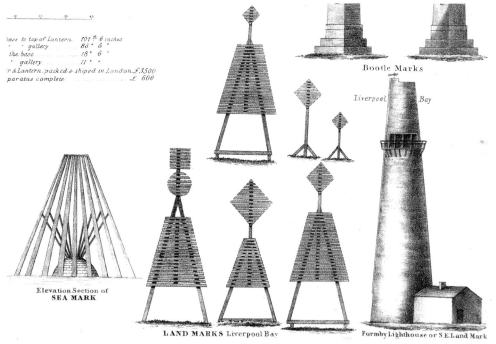

base to top of Lantern ..... 101 ft 6 inches
" " gallery .... 80 " 6 "
the base .... 18 " 6 "
" gallery .... 11 " "
r & Lantern, packed & shiped in London £3500
paratus complete .... £ 600

Elevation Section of
SEA MARK

Bootle Marks

Liverpool Bay

LAND MARKS Liverpool Bay

Formby Lighthouse or S.E.Land Mark

IN-045

IN-046

IN-045. British unlighted beacons (day-marks). 1846. Gen. Coll., plate 25, volume of plates accompanying the *Report . . . on improvements in the light-house system . . .*, Senate doc. no. 488, 29:1.

The original Tybee daymark may have looked like one of these British models from the early nineteenth century.

IN-046. Yerba Buena Lighthouse, Yerba Buena (Goat) Island, San Francisco, California. Ca. 1910. P&P, HABS, CAL, 38-SANFRA,130-1.

opposite
IN-047. Charlevoix Light and harbor entrance, Charlevoix, Michigan. 1900–1910. DPCC, LC-D4-36405.

This rectangular, pyramidal lighthouse on posts was made of wood. It was built for Charlevoix North Pier and went into operation in 1885.

IN-048. Lyndoe, or Lyndoc, Island Light, Gananoque Narrows, Thousand Islands, St. Lawrence River, Canada. 1890–1901. DPCC, LC-D4-8809.

A wooden Canadian lighthouse of the type that used to be found in the United States.

IN-049. Prospect Harbor Point Light and keeper's dwelling, Prospect Harbor, Maine. Richard Cheek, photographer, 1990. P&P, HABS, ME-201-1.

In a reversal of the usual pattern, this 1891 wooden tower replaced an earlier granite tower attached to a dwelling.

IN-050. Prospect Harbor Point Lighthouse, Prospect Harbor, Maine. Richard Cheek, photographer, 1990. P&P, HABS, ME-201-1.

sea level in 1854. When the raised height proved insufficient, a new brick tower was erected (lighted in 1870) with a light 192 feet above sea level, making it at the time, and still, the tallest tower in the United States (see 2-016–2-027). Many other tall towers followed, most on the low-lying shores of the southern East Coast.

Wood was another standard construction material for early towers. One of the first colonial aids to navigation was a wooden daymark at Tybee Island built by the colony of Georgia. It stood 90 feet tall and had an open base and siding at the top (IN-045). Destroyed in a storm, it was replaced with another equally tall wooden tower, and this second one may have had a lamp. The third Tybee Island structure, completed in 1773, was a brick octagonal lighthouse.

A tendency to replace wooden towers with ones made of more durable and less combustible materials has left us with few freestanding wooden lighthouses. The oldest surviving wooden tower is Gurnet Point Lighthouse (1843) in Plymouth, Massachusetts, successor to a colonial-era lighthouse, which had been America's first twin lights (IN-001). It has an octagonal shape and stands 34 feet tall; its twin was dismantled in 1924. Yet there are some instances of wooden towers built late in the nineteenth century (IN-046–IN-055).

An early form of lighthouse structure, made of wood as well as masonry, was the cottage-style lighthouse, which consisted of a dwelling and integral tower. The tower could be placed in the middle of the building, at one of the ends but within the walls, or attached to a wall of the dwelling. While these towers were not very tall, they could have high focal planes when placed on promontories. Many of the first California lighthouses were of this type: Old

IN-051

IN-052

IN-053

IN-051. Perkins Island Lighthouse, near Georgetown, Maine. Richard Cheek, photographer, 1989. P&P, HABS, ME-190-4.

Perkins Island Lighthouse, built in 1898, is another example of a late wood-frame lighthouse.

IN-052. Perkins Island Lighthouse and keeper's dwelling, near Georgetown, Maine. Richard Cheek, photographer, 1989. P&P, HABS, ME-190-3.

IN-053. Inside looking up at the roof of Perkins Island Lighthouse, near Georgetown, Maine. Richard Cheek, photographer, 1989. P&P, HABS, ME-190-5.

IN-054

IN-055

IN-054. This little wooden lighthouse was one of the Kennebec River Range Lights (1908), Arrowsic, Maine. Richard Cheek, photographer, 1989. P&P, HABS, ME,12-AROW,2-3.

IN-055. Inside looking up, Kennebec River Range Lights (1908), Arrowsic, Maine. Richard Cheek, photographer, 1989. P&P, HABS, ME,12-AROW,2-5.

IN-056. East front of Old Point Loma Light, built 1855, near San Diego, California. Early twentieth century. P&P, HABS, CAL,37-POLO,1-4.

IN-056

Point Loma Lighthouse (1855; IN-056) near San Diego is a stone and brick structure, while the ornate Mare Island Lighthouse (1873, no longer extant; IN-057), once at the eastern end of San Pablo Bay, and its architecturally similar neighbor, East Brother Island Lighthouse (1874), were both built of wood (IN-058).

The 1840s saw the introduction of an important new construction material for lighthouses: iron. This material was used in two ways: in iron plates, and in piles—the "legs" of lighthouses. The first all-iron lighthouse was the iron-plate type, a technology devel-

IN-057. Mare Island Lighthouse, Mare Island, California. 1872. Gen. Coll., *Annual Report of the Light-House Board*, 1872.

IN-058. Lighthouse, Waukegan Vic., Illinois. P&P, HABS, ILL,49-WAUK-2-.

IN-057

IN-058

oped by British engineers and commonly used for their colonial lighthouses. The structures could be conical, cylindrical, or octagonal; they were made of cast-iron plates bolted together and usually lined with brick. The Long Island Head Lighthouse in Boston Harbor (1844) was the first such tower in the United States. Because they weighed less than masonry towers of similar dimensions, were durable, and could be prefabricated, the cast-iron plate lighthouses were especially well suited for piers (see Section Four).

Another form of iron lighthouse introduced at the end of the 1840s was the iron skeleton or pile lighthouse. Designed to solve the problem of how to build a permanent structure on shifting bottoms and water-covered sites, the lighthouse consisted of an open

IN-059

IN-059. Tall iron skeleton lighthouse at Fowey Rocks, off Key Biscayne, Florida. Ca. 1893. Gen. Coll., *Annual Report of the Light-House Board*, 1894.

IN-060. Typical nineteenth-century cottage-style skeleton lighthouse, unidentified name and location. William Henry Jackson, photographer, 1895. WTCPC, LC-D426-791.

(skeleton) frame, made of piles, or posts, fixed into the ground that supported a dwelling, storage space, watch-room, and lantern. The solid parts were raised above the highest expected level of the water; thus, the waves could wash through the legs without resistance, and the narrow profile of the piles in the ground minimized erosion at the base. Like the cast-iron plate lighthouses, the skeleton lighthouses had the advantage of being comparatively light and could be prefabricated. The earliest examples of skeleton lighthouses, built in the late 1840s, were all placed on submerged or wave-washed sites. While the details of their foundation piles vary—straight pile, screw pile, disk pile—these lighthouses roughly fall into two categories: tall towers and small towers. The Fowey Rocks Lighthouse in Florida (1878) is an example of a tall tower (IN-059). The small towers were essentially cottage-style lighthouses on stilts (IN-060). Many of the small type were built along the Chesapeake Bay and shores of other bays and rivers. Beginning in the 1860s, the first skeleton towers were built on land. In these cases, the dwellings and ancillary buildings were separate from the lighthouse tower.

Other types of foundations were introduced for water-covered sites or soft ground that could withstand battering from ice in spring thaws better than the iron-pile foundations. An early type was the crib foundation, consisting of a timber frame filled with rocks, such as were used to build wharves. Another traditional form, the stone pier,

IN-061

IN-062

IN-061. Southwest Ledge Lighthouse, Long Island Sound, near New Haven, Connecticut. 1876. Gen. Coll., *Annual Report of the Light-House Board*, 1876.

IN-062. Molokai (Kalaupapa) Lighthouse seen from the west-northwest, Kalaupapa Peninsula, Hawaii. Jack E. Boucher, photographer, 1991. P&P, HABS, HI,3-KALA.V,5-A-3.

served as a base for lighthouses. The 1870s saw the introduction of the iron tubular foundation, made of a large metal cylinder called a caisson. Tradesmen built the caissons on land and towed them to the site, where they were sunk and their interiors filled with concrete. It was possible to erect any type of lighthouse on these elevated platforms or piers. Iron-plate lighthouses are often found on iron caissons; in these cases, the iron plating of the foundation extends up to the superstructure. While this usually resulted in a simple, cylindrical superstructure, some lighthouses on iron caissons were architecturally ornate. An example is the Southwest Ledge (New Haven Breakwater) Lighthouse (1877) in Long Island Sound near the entrance to New Haven Harbor (IN-061).

In the twentieth century, new construction materials often led to changes in the traditional shapes of lighthouses. Reinforced concrete allowed buildings to be built tall yet stable without having wide bases; thus, they have vertical or nearly vertical walls rather than a conical shape. The first reinforced concrete lighthouse, the Point Arena Lighthouse in California, was built in 1908 to replace an earlier lighthouse that was destroyed in the great San Francisco earthquake of 1906. An example of a nearly straight-

IN-063

IN-063. View of Split Rock Lighthouse on its promontory, Two Harbors Vic., Minnesota. Jet Lowe, photographer, 1990. HAER, MINN,38-TWOHA.V,1-1.

IN-064. Elevation of a lighthouse and shaft, wrought iron. Ca. 1851. Gen. Coll., *Report of the Officers Constituting the Light-House Board . . . Under the Act of March 3, 1851* (Washington, DC: 1852).

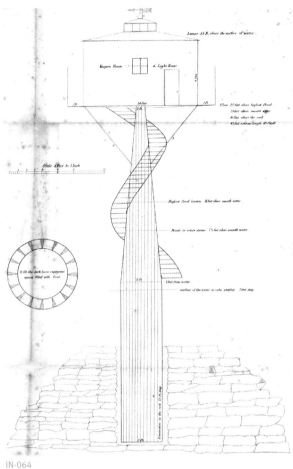

IN-064

sided concrete tower is the Molokai Lighthouse in Hawaii, built in 1909 (IN-062). Several Hawaiian lighthouses were concrete.

Skeleton-frame construction, the technology used to build skyscrapers, consists of a metal interior frame and exterior cladding, and it was adopted for lighthouse construction. The Split Rock Lighthouse, built in 1910 on the northern shore of Lake Superior near Two Harbors, Minnesota, has a metal frame covered with brick and concrete curtain walls. Yet the octagonal, "brick" lighthouse that resulted has a traditional, and very picturesque, appearance (IN-063).

A recent type of lighthouse, dating from the 1960s, is the Texas Tower, so named because it resembles the offshore platforms used for drilling for oil along the Texas coast (see 7-017). While it departs drastically from traditional lighthouse forms, it could be considered an updated version of the skeleton pile lighthouses. The first to be completed was in Buzzard's Bay in 1961. Only six towers of this type have been constructed.

The special problems of certain sites and the introduction of new construction technologies led engineers to conceive some interesting solutions for lighthouses that were never executed. Iron inspired many valuable new kinds of foundations and lighthouse forms, but one idea that was not implemented was an iron lighthouse atop an iron shaft, reached by a spiral stairway (IN-064). The shaft was designed to be 5 feet in diameter, at most 42 feet long, and sunk like a pile 12 feet deep into rock. The keeper's room was to be 14 feet in diameter and 8 feet high, with a small lantern and lamps at the top. Although simple and ingenious, this design apparently was not practical.

The sections that follow trace how lighthouse structures and the materials for constructing them have changed over time in response to changes in the administration of America's lighthouse system and evolving technology. Several different lighthouses may have been erected at a single site (an early one replaced with one or more later towers) or original towers were altered: raised in height or sometimes lowered, their lanterns removed, or moved from their original positions when erosion threatened to undermine them. Lighthouses were built to be used. We may see them as noble and picturesque, and many are of fine proportions and excellent workmanship; but during their working lives, they were treated as utilitarian structures. Many were demolished or their associated structures—dwelling, oil houses, and so on—removed, once their service was no longer needed. Thus, some of the lighthouses illustrated in this book are no longer standing. The National Park Service, local governments, and private groups, such as lighthouse preservation and historical societies, have stepped up to preserve many of the old lighthouses, so these "steadfast, serene, immovable" structures will exist to inspire future generations.

NOTE

In this book, if only one date is given for a lighthouse, it is the date the structure went into operation; if more than one date is given, they are the years during which it was constructed. Readers should keep in mind that even though one date may be given, many lighthouses took several years to build. For example, Minot's Ledge Lighthouse (IN-043), a sea-rock lighthouse located over a mile from land, took six years to construct

(1855–1860). Offshore lighthouses like this one were the most arduous and time-consuming structures to erect. Tower heights given here are based on the best available information and are for the tower excluding the lantern, unless stated otherwise. Some sources measure tower heights from the ground to the top of the tower, and some from the ground to the top of the lantern. Thus, sources often disagree about height and may not specify whether or not the lantern is included.

STONE AND

1764–1852

BRICK TOWERS

Stone and brick were the most commonly used materials for building light-houses. They also were used for a longer time than any other material, starting with the first known North American lighthouse, Boston Light (see IN-042), and continuing into the second decade of the twentieth century. While wood was also used at an early date, the obvious fire hazard of operating flaming lamps in a wooden structure, and the harsh weather conditions to which lighthouses were exposed, made masonry the material of choice. Stone was preferred over brick for colonial-era lighthouses. Until the second half of the nineteenth century, bricks were handmade and therefore a fairly expensive construction material. Stone found in the vicinity of a lighthouse site might be a less expensive option. In the early lighthouses, the stone was left rough (called rubble) and finished with a layer of stucco. Some of the more handsome (and costly) lighthouses used dressed stone, which has a smooth surface. Where suitable stone was unavailable or too expensive, designers used brick.

The defining structural characteristic of the masonry towers is their bearing walls. The walls were built with various materials and construction methods, including solid blocks of stone, stone facing with rubble and brick backing, solid brick, and brick interior and exterior faces with a hollow space or rubble filling in between. A common feature is that they are "bearing," meaning that each layer of masonry supports the layers above it (1-001). The walls therefore are in compression; and because the load is greater at the bottom than at the top, they generally taper upward from a thicker base to a thinner top. This structural characteristic, as well as the greater stability of a structure with a wide base relative to its top, account for the familiar conical and pyramidal shapes of many towers. British lighthouse engineers, following the example of John Smeaton's landmark Eddystone Lighthouse (1759; 1-002–1-003), built flared bases for tall towers—giving them a profile like the trunk of an oak tree—in the belief that this form was necessary for the structure's stability. American lighthouse engineers did not adopt this detail.

While stone may be more durable than wood, many early masonry towers did not prove permanent. Some types of stone weather badly, and of course lighthouses are exposed to particularly harsh conditions. For example, wind and blowing sand have eaten away the stone walls of the original Cape Henry Lighthouse (1792), leaving the face of the tower badly deteriorated (1-009). Even if the towers survived scouring sand and storms, their foundations could be undermined by erosion, which has claimed many a lighthouse. And while the walls of masonry towers are noncombustible, early lighthouses had wooden interior stairways and finishes, which sometimes caught fire and caused damage. Indeed, considering their hard use and harsh settings, it is remarkable that any lighthouses from the first half of the nineteenth century survive.

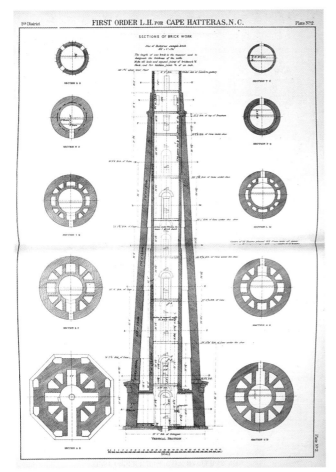

1-001

1-002

1-003

1-001. Drawing showing vertical and horizontal sections of the brick-work, Cape Hatteras Lighthouse, north of Cape Hatteras Point/Outer Banks, North Carolina. Julius Bien, engraver, 1869. Gen. Coll., *Specifications for a Light-House to be Erected at Cape Hatteras, North Carolina* (Washington, DC: G.P.O., 1869).

America's tallest lighthouse, the second Cape Hatteras Lighthouse (1870), has straight, hollow walls, with radiating tie-walls connecting the interior and exterior walls.

1-002. Eddystone Lighthouse, Plymouth, England, from View of England in the Photochrom print collection. Ca. 1890–1900. LC-DIG-ppmsc-08791.

Stump of John Smeaton's Eddystone Lighthouse (1759) and the fourth and current Eddystone Lighthouse (1882), both with profiles patterned on oak tree trunks, flaring out at the bottom.

1-003. Bell Rock Lighthouse during a storm, Scotland. Engraving by J. Horsburgh after drawing by J. M. W. Turner, 1824. P&P, LC-USZ62-70955.

PYRAMIDAL TOWERS

A number of the colonial-era towers were octagonal pyramids. Most were made of stone, like the Cape Henlopen Lighthouse in Delaware (1767, 1-008). This 69-foot-tall tower served as a model for some of the first lighthouses built by the U.S. government. Another, the Tybee Island tower in Georgia (1773), probably was made of brick. These two are no longer standing. Among the other early towers of this type that have not survived are the first Bald Head lighthouse (1795), a brick tower that was lost to erosion in 1817, and the first Cape Hatteras lighthouse in North Carolina (1803), a granite tower that was demolished after the second tower was completed. Fortunately, some of the pyramidal lighthouses from the early national period, as well as one from the colonial period, are still standing.

1-004. South view, exterior of Sandy Hook Lighthouse, Sandy Hook, New Jersey. Nathaniel R. Ewan, photographer, 1937. P&P, HABS, NJ,13-SANHO,2-2.

Sandy Hook Lighthouse, New Jersey

Originally known as New York Lighthouse, the Sandy Hook Light in New Jersey marks the southern entrance to New York Harbor. Completed in 1764, it is the only surviving colonial-era tower. It is built of rubble stone and was described in the year it was lighted as being 103 feet tall to the top of the lantern, with a 29-foot-diameter base and a 15-foot-diameter top. Unlike many other lighthouses, its dimensions have not changed over time. The 85-foot-tall tower (not counting the lantern) today has a cylindrical interior of brick, which was added in 1863 along with an iron spiral stairway. The exterior has been whitewashed. Isaac Conro of New York City was the builder.

1-004

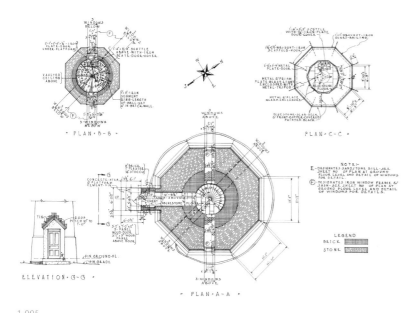

1-005

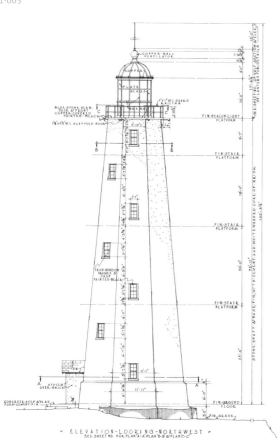

1-006

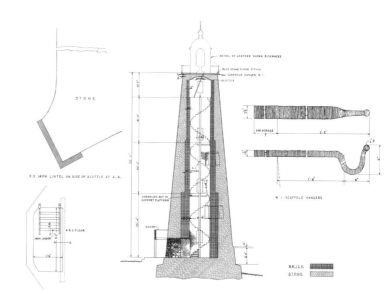

1-007

1-005. Horizontal sections Sandy Hook Lighthouse, Sandy Hook, New Jersey. Robert A. Mackellar, delineator, 1937. P&P, HABS, NJ,13-SANHO,2-, sheet no. 2.

1-006. Elevation, Sandy Hook Lighthouse looking northwest, Sandy Hook, New Jersey. Robert A. Mackellar, delineator, 1937. P&P, HABS, NJ,13-SANHO,2-, sheet no. 3.

1-007. Vertical section through to Sandy Hook Lighthouse tower, Sandy Hook, New Jersey. Samuel Tilton, delineator, 1937. P&P, HABS, NJ,13-SANHO,2-, sheet no. 4.

Cape Henlopen Lighthouse, Delaware

Marking the entrance to the Delaware Bay, Cape Henlopen Lighthouse (1767) was a 69-foot-tall tower that tapered from a 26-foot-diameter base to 17 1/2 feet in diameter at the top. It survived into the twentieth century but collapsed in 1926, a casualty of shore erosion. Photos of it are scarce.

1-008

1-008. Cape Henlopen Lighthouse, Delaware. Copyright N. L. Stebbins, ca. 1891. P&P, LC-USZ62-92461.

John McComb Jr.'s Lighthouses

Two lighthouses, Cape Charles and Cape Henry, flank the entrance to the Chesapeake Bay, the former on the north side and the latter on the south side, near Virginia Beach, Virginia. In colonial times, Virginia attempted to erect a lighthouse at Cape Henry, but little progress had been made by the time the Revolutionary War started. The lighthouse act of 1789, which authorized the federal government to assume responsibility for lighthouses, provided for a lighthouse near the entrance of the Chesapeake Bay, and the Cape Henry site was chosen.

The contract to build the lighthouse went to John McComb Jr., an important builder, surveyor, and architect in New York City. Like its model, Cape Henlopen Light, Cape Henry Light was an octagonal, pyramidal tower with stone walls, but at roughly 92 feet tall it was about 20 feet taller than the Cape Henlopen structure. Nevertheless, the diameters of its base and top were similar. It was first lighted in 1792. The stone used in the tower was sandstone from two different sources. The lower part of the tower is Acquia stone, which was cheap and easy to work but has not held up well. The upper part is red sandstone, which is better wearing. The lighthouse was abandoned when cracks developed in the tower; although deactivated in 1881, it was left standing and survives to this day.

McComb went on to design two architecturally similar lighthouses: Montauk Point (1797) and Eatons Neck (1799), both on Long Island Sound in New York. Montauk Point Light, standing on a bluff at the eastern end of the island, had walls of hammered sandstone and originally stood 80 feet tall. In 1860 the tower height was raised to 110 feet, giving it a focal plane of about 168 feet above sea level.

1-009. Cape Henry lighthouses, new tower (left) 1881 and old tower (right) 1792, Virginia Beach, Virginia. Ca. 1905. DPCC, LC-D4-18400.

1-010. Old Cape Henry Lighthouse, Virginia Beach, Virginia. Associated Press Photo, 1929. P&P, NYWTS, SUBJ/GEOG: LIGHTHOUSES—CAPE HENRY—VIRGINIA.

1-009

1-010

1-011

1-012

1-011. Keeper Charles Schumacher and his family on Thanksgiving Day at Montauk Point Lighthouse, Long Island, New York. Roger Higgins, photographer, 1958. P&P, NYWTS, SUBJ/GEOG: LIGHTHOUSES– MONTAUK–MONTAUK POINT, L.I.

1-012. Montauk Point Lighthouse illuminated again after being blacked out during World War II, Long Island, New York. Coast Guard Photo, 1945. P&P, NYWTS, SUBJ/GEOG: LIGHTHOUSES– MONTAUK–MONTAUK POINT, L.I.

New London Harbor Lighthouse, Connecticut

The second New London Harbor Lighthouse, first lighted in 1801, is a brown sandstone tower that replaced a colonial-era stone lighthouse built in 1760. Standing about 89 feet tall, it was built by Abisha Woodward, who also built the pyramidal Faulkner's Island Light off Guilford, Connecticut, a year later and previously had built the first Bald Head Island Light in North Carolina.

1-013. New London Harbor Lighthouse, New London, Connecticut. Ca. 1900. P&P, LC-USZ62-127104.

1-014. New London Harbor Lighthouse, New London, Connecticut. Standard Oil Co., New Jersey, 1952. P&P, NYWTS, SUBJ/GEOG: LIGHTHOUSES–PEQUOT POINT–NEW LONDON, CONN., detail.

1-013

1-014

Old Point Comfort Lighthouse, Virginia

1-015. Old Point Comfort Lighthouse, Fort Monroe, Hampton, Virginia. Jack E. Boucher, photographer, 1988. P&P, HABS, VA,28-HAMP,2J-2.

1-016. South elevation, Old Point Comfort Lighthouse, Fort Monroe, Hampton, Virginia. Jack E. Boucher, photographer, 1988. P&P, HABS, VA,28-HAMP,2J-4.

Another early pyramidal structure, Old Point Comfort Lighthouse was built near Fort Monroe, north of Cape Henry Light at the entrance to Hampton Roads. Lighted in 1802, it has sandstone walls and stands about 54 feet tall. Its interior stairway is made of stone rather than wood. Work began on the architecturally similar New Point Comfort Lighthouse just after the Old Point Comfort Lighthouse was completed. Located on a point farther north up the Chesapeake Bay and finished in 1805, it too is sandstone and measures about 58 feet tall. The stonemason Elzy Burroughs designed and constructed both towers and became the first keeper of the New Point Comfort Light.

1-015

1-016

Sands Point Lighthouse, New York

This Long Island Sound lighthouse, built in 1809, is a brown sandstone tower that stands 65 feet tall.

1-017. Sands Point Lighthouse, North Hempstead, New York. David Sharpe, photographer, 1974. P&P, HAER, NY,30-HEMPN, 2-1.

1-017

Cedar Point Lighthouse, Massachusetts

Lighting the entrance to Scituate Harbor, this tower started out in 1811 as a roughly 22-foot-tall stone octagon. Later a brick extension was added to its top, bringing it to a little over 40 feet tall. The extension accounts for the structure's unusual shape. The lighthouse was abandoned for many years, and the lantern currently on the building is a reconstruction.

1-018

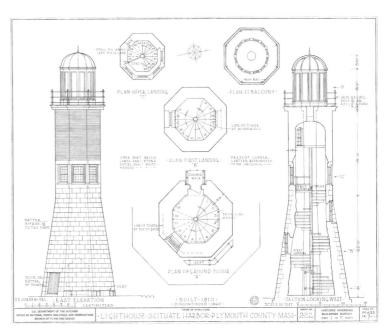

1-019

1-018. View of Cedar Point Lighthouse from the southeast, Scituate, Massachusetts. Arthur C. Haskell, photographer, 1934. P&P, HABS, MASS,12-SCIT.V,1-2.

1-019. Elevation, section, and plans of Cedar Point Lighthouse from the southeast, Scituate, Massachusetts. E. E. Jordan, delineator, 1934. P&P, HABS, MASS,12-SCIT.V,1-, sheet no. 1.

1-020. Elevations of Cedar Point Lighthouse from the southeast, Scituate, Massachusetts. C. Vaughn Holmes, delineator, 1934. P&P, HABS, MASS,12-SCIT.V,1-.

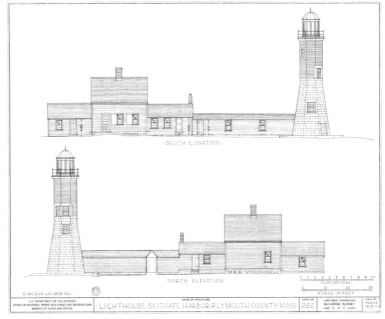

1-020

Charlotte-Genessee Lighthouse, New York

Completed in 1822, this 40-foot-tall lighthouse was built of rubble stone.

1-021

1-022

1-021. Southwest view, Charlotte-Genessee Lighthouse, Rochester, New York. Walter H. Cassebeer, photographer, 1936. P&P, HABS, NY,28-ROCH,10-2.

1-022. Section, south elevation, and roof of Charlotte-Genessee Lighthouse, Rochester, New York. Herbert A. Lawrence, delineator, 1936. P&P, HABS, NY,28-ROCH,10-, sheet no. 2.

Buffalo Harbor Light, New York

1-023. Buffalo Harbor Lighthouse from the southeast, after it was raised. Copy of photograph from the Buffalo and Erie County Historical Society, 1859. P&P, HABS, NY,15-BUF,17-1.

Buffalo Harbor Lighthouse, completed in 1833, was a 44-foot-tall tower made of limestone, with stone stairs and landings. It measured 20 feet in diameter at its base and tapered to 12 feet at the top. Iron bands were built into the walls to counteract their spreading. In 1857–1858 it was raised about 6 feet and received a new lens. As in other pier lighthouses, the keeper's house was separate from the tower, located on land.

1-023

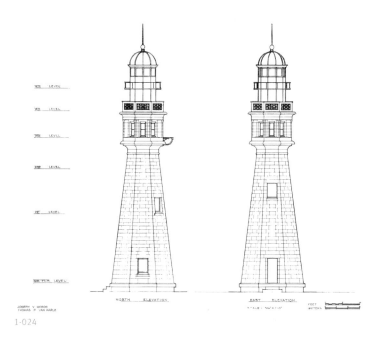

1-024

1-025

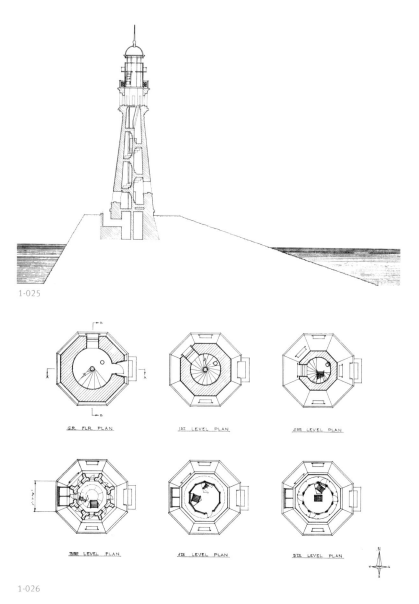

1-026

1-024. North and east elevations, Buffalo Harbor Lighthouse, Buffalo, New York. Joseph V. Morog and Thomas F. Van Aarle, delineator, 1960. P&P, HABS, NY,15-BUF,17-, sheet no. 4.

1-025. Section through Buffalo Harbor Lighthouse showing foundation and probable location of the oil vault, Buffalo, New York. Joseph V. Morog and Thomas F. Van Aarle, delineators, 1960. P&P, HABS, NY,15-BUF,17-, sheet no. 6.

1-026. Horizontal sections through Buffalo Harbor Lighthouse, Buffalo, New York. Joseph V. Morog and Thomas F. Van Aarle, delineators, 1960. P&P, HABS, NY,15-BUF,17-, sheet no. 2.

1-027. Buffalo Harbor Lighthouse and look-out tower, with the steamboat *Juniata* passing, Buffalo, New York. Between 1910 and 1920. DPCC, LC-D4-72733.

The lighthouse is the building on the right. The square, pyramidal tower in the foreground was a lookout tower.

1-028. Buffalo Harbor Lighthouse, Buffalo, New York. Ca. 1900. DPCC, LC-D4-12920.

1-027

1-028

Oswego Harbor Light, New York

This gray stone tower was built at the end of west pier in Oswego Harbor in 1836. The tower was raised 14 feet in 1869. It became the inner harbor light when a second light was built on a new breakwater. It is no longer standing.

1-029. Oswego Harbor Light and Fort Ontario, Oswego, New York. Ca. 1900. DPCC, LC-D4-12161.

1-029

Lynde Point (Saybrook Harbor) Lighthouse, Connecticut

1-030. Lynde Point (Saybrook Harbor) Lighthouse, Old Saybrook, Connecticut. P&P, SSF, LIGHTHOUSES—CONNECTICUT, OLD SAYBROOK.

First lighted in 1839, this brown sandstone tower stands 65 feet tall. It is painted white. Its predecessor was a wooden pyramidal tower.

1-030

Five Mile Point (Old New Haven Harbor) Lighthouse, Connecticut

Another octagonal pyramid in Connecticut, Five Mile Point Light went into service in 1847 and replaced an earlier wooden tower. Built by Marcus Bassett, it stands 70 feet tall and has brown sandstone walls and an interior stairway of granite. It was deactivated in 1877.

1-031. Five Mile Point (Old New Haven Harbor) Lighthouse, New Haven, Connecticut. Ca. 1900. DPCC, LC-D4-13687.

1-032. Five Mile Point (Old New Haven Harbor) Lighthouse, New Haven, Connecticut. Between 1901 and 1906. DPCC, LC-D4-9040.

1-031

1-032

Point Judith, Rhode Island

1-033. Point Judith Lighthouse. WC, P&P, SSF, LIGHTHOUSES—RHODE ISLAND, NARRAGANSETT, POINT JUDITH LIGHT.

Completed in 1857 on the western side of the entrance to Narragansett Bay, Point Judith Lighthouse is a brown sandstone tower that stands 51 feet tall. It replaced two earlier towers.

1-033

Sabine Pass Lighthouse, Louisiana

This lighthouse is an octagonal tower, but its unique base gives it an unusual appearance. Its walls taper very little, and to keep the nearly cylindrical structure upright on the soft, low-lying ground, its base is reinforced with eight buttresses. Completed in 1857, the Sabine Pass Lighthouse is 75 feet tall and made of brick, with brick and concrete buttresses.

1-034. Sabine Pass Lighthouse, Sabine Pass, Louisiana. P&P, S, lot 13468.

1-034

Crown Point Light, New York

1-035. Crown Point Light, Lake Champlain, New York. Ca. 1907. DPCC, LC-D4-19881.

Similar to its neighbors on Lake Champlain, Point Au Roche and Windmill Point lighthouses, Crown Point Light was a 55-foot-tall gray limestone tower that went into service in 1859. It has been replaced with a memorial to Samuel de Champlain (1912). The other two—in New York and Vermont, respectively—survive.

1-035

Lighthouse at Sault Ste. Marie, Michigan

This pyramidal tower appears to be masonry.

1-036

Boston Harbor Lighthouse, Massachusetts

1-037. Logo of the Boston Marine Society, showing the sun shining on a ship sailing into Boston Harbor past the 1716 lighthouse. Dates from the eighteenth century. Gen. Coll., R. G. F. Candage, "Boston Light and the Brewsters," *New England Magazine* 13 (October 1895): 132.

Although it stands on the site of the first lighthouse in North America, today's Boston Light is the second tower—a replacement for one blown up by the British as they evacuated Boston in the early days of the Revolutionary War. The original tower (1716) had survived two serious fires before its violent demise. It was conical, built of brick with a wooden lantern, and stood about 65 feet tall, or 75 feet to the top of the lantern (see IN-042).

The second Boston Light, completed in 1783, also is conical and about the same height as its predecessor, but it is built of stone. When first completed, the base measured 25 feet in diameter and the top of the tower measured 15 feet. The walls were a sturdy 7 1/2 feet thick at the base and decreased to 2 1/2 feet at the top, which formed a cylindrical interior about 10 feet in diameter. The original lantern was octagonal and contained four oil lamps. The lighthouse was ceded to the United States in 1790. In 1856 a new, revolving lighting apparatus was installed, and four years later the tower was raised to 98 feet.

1-037

1-038

1-039

Portland Head Lighthouse, Maine

An old lighthouse of classic conical form in a picturesque setting, Portland Head Lighthouse has stood for over 200 years in Cape Elizabeth, Maine, marking Portland Harbor. Construction on this lighthouse began in 1787 under the auspices of the Commonwealth of Massachusetts, which then controlled the area that became Maine. The federal government took over the lighthouse in 1790, and it was lighted in January 1791. Since it was actually lighted before Cape Henry Lighthouse, it has the distinction of being the first new, federally owned lighthouse. John Nichols and Jonathan Bryant, master builders of Portland, designed and erected the building. The tower is about 80 feet to the lantern deck, on a 24-foot-diameter base.

The height of the tower has been raised and lowered over the years. When the tower was completed in 1790, it reportedly stood about 72 feet tall, but in 1813 orders were given to reduce it by 25 feet. Then, in 1865, funds were appropriated to raise the tower. This was not the end of the changes: in 1883 the tower height was lowered 21 feet. But mariners protested, so in 1885 the tower was raised again to its present height. All these changes left the tower a mix of materials: the first 44 feet of the walls are rough granite blocks, followed by about 20 feet of brick above a granite coping, and then an iron cylinder. The interior is lined with brick. The tower is painted white.

1-040

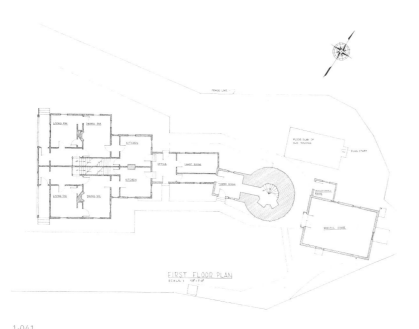

1-041

1-041. Portland Head Lighthouse, first floor plan showing the tower and associated structures, Cape Elizabeth, Maine. Davis L. Jahncke Jr., delineator, 1965. P&P, HABS, ME,3-CAPEL,2-, sheet no. 2.

1-042. Southeast elevation, Portland Head Lighthouse, Cape Elizabeth, Maine. Davis L. Jahncke Jr., delineator, 1965. P&P, HABS, ME,3-CAPEL,2-, sheet no. 3.

1-043. Portland Head Lighthouse showing its headland, Cape Elizabeth, Maine. Ca. 1917. LC-USZ62-101998.

1-042

1-043

1-044. Detail of lantern, Portland Head Lighthouse, Cape Elizabeth, Maine. Jack E. Boucher, photographer, 1965. P&P, HABS, ME,3-CAPEL,2-6.

1-045. Portland Head Lighthouse, Cape Elizabeth, Maine. Ca. 1902. DPCC, LC-D4-16152.

1-046. Portland Head Lighthouse, Cape Elizabeth, Maine. Ralph F. Blood, photographer, ca. 1931. LC-USZ62-101999.

1-045

1-044

1-046

Great Point Lighthouse, Massachusetts

Replacing an eighteenth-century lighthouse, the second Great Point Lighthouse was built in 1818. A complex of buildings developed around this stone tower. In 1984 the lighthouse was destroyed in a storm, but by then the lighthouse had been recorded by the Historic American Building Survey (HABS). A new lighthouse—a replica of the stone tower—was erected in 1986 three hundred yards west of the previous tower.

1-047. Great Point Lighthouse, Nantucket County, Massachusetts. John F. Murphy, photographer, 1897. P&P, HABS, MASS,10-NANT,73-8.

1-047

1-048. Great Point Lighthouse looking east, Nantucket County, Massachusetts. Jack E. Boucher, photographer, 1969. P&P, HABS, MASS,10-NANT,73-3.

1-049. Great Point Lighthouse, interior showing the ground floor with spiral iron stair and niches, Nantucket County, Massachusetts. Jack E. Boucher, photographer, 1969. P&P, HABS, MASS,10-NANT,73-5

1-050. South elevation, Great Point Lighthouse, Nantucket County, Massachusetts. Edward Bondi, delineator, 1969. P&P, HABS, MASS,10-NANT,73-.

1-048

1-049

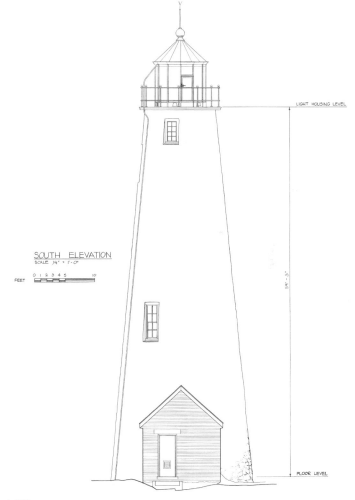

SOUTH ELEVATION
SCALE 1/4" = 1'-0"

FEET 0 1 2 3 4 5   10

1-050

Burnt Island Light, Maine

The second-oldest extant lighthouse in Maine, and one of the oldest lighthouses still in original condition, Burnt Island Light is a small, conical masonry tower, an example of a type found on the islands and headlands of Maine. Standing at the entrance to Booth Bay Harbor, the stone tower is 30 feet tall and went into service in 1821. Like many other Maine lighthouses, it is painted white.

1-051. Burnt Island Lighthouse, Burnt Island, Southport, Maine. Richard Cheek, photographer, 1991. P&P, HABS, ME-219-5.

1-051

1-052. Burnt Island Lighthouse and keeper's dwelling, Burnt Island, Southport, Maine. Richard Cheek, photographer, 1991. P&P, HABS, ME-219-3.

1-053. Stairway inside Burnt Island Lighthouse, Burnt Island, Southport, Maine. Richard Cheek, photographer, 1991. P&P, HABS, ME-219-7.

1-052

1-053

Frank's Island Light, Louisiana

The federal government built several lighthouses to mark the entrances to passes through the Mississippi delta to the Mississippi River: Northeast Pass, South Pass, and Southwest Pass. Frank's Island Light, the earliest lighthouse in the area, marked the Northeast Pass. Designed by architect-engineer B. Henry Latrobe and his son Henry S. B. Latrobe, the plans called for a monumental tower in which the keeper would live. It was to have a stone colonnade and platform at the base, a stone staircase, and brick walls covered with plaster. To support this massive structure on its marshy site, a foundation was made of piles covered with a timber grillage filled with shells and other hard material and grout. The lighthouse was completed in 1819 at a cost of around $85,000, making it the most expensive American lighthouse of the time. But it began to fail immediately. Henry S. B.

1-054

Latrobe planned a new tower that apparently replicated the original design and made use of materials from the old tower. Winslow Lewis, a major lighthouse builder, was the contractor. The new tower went into operation in 1823. As executed, the tower did not contain a stone staircase; whether it had all the other architectural features of its predecessor is unknown because it sank, eventually about 20 feet, into the marsh. In 1856, when the Pass à L'Outre Lighthouse (in Louisiana) went into operation, Frank's Island Light was discontinued. Although the lighthouse failed structurally, it was an important lighthouse in its day; and given the marshy site, building it represented a technological achievement.

1-054. Frank's Island Light viewed from the north, North East Pass, Mississippi River, Louisiana. Samuel Wilson Jr., photographer, 1934. P&P, HABS, LA,38-_____,1-2.

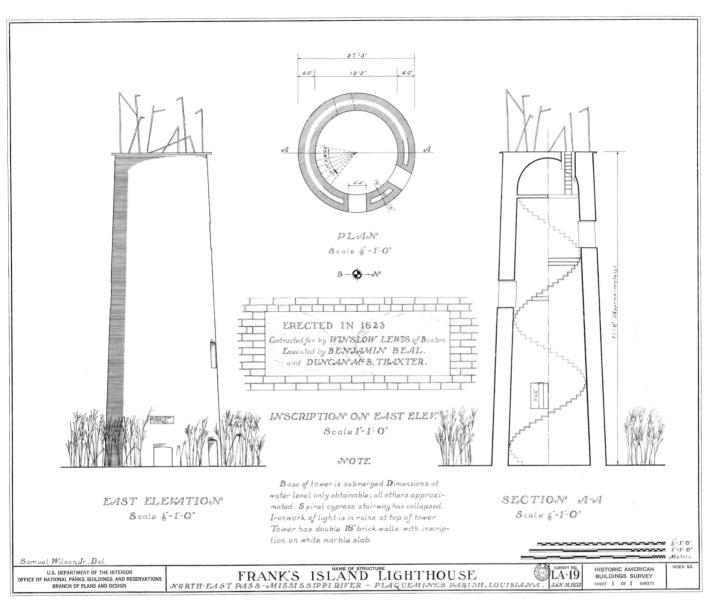

27'-3"

4'-0" 19'-3" 4'-0"

PLAN
Scale ⅛"=1'-0"

S ◆ N

4'-4"

A — A

ERECTED IN 1823
Contracted for by WINSLOW LEWIS of Boston
Executed by BENJAMIN BEAL.
and DUNCAN MᶜB. THAXTER.

INSCRIPTION ON EAST ELEV.
Scale 1"=1'-0"

NOTE

Base of tower is submerged. Dimensions at
water level only obtainable; all others approxi-
mated. Spiral cypress stairway has collapsed.
Ironwork of light is in ruins at top of tower.
Tower has double 18" brick walls with inscription on white marble slab.

EAST ELEVATION
Scale ⅛"=1'-0"

SECTION A-A
Scale ⅛"=1'-0"

71'-6" (Approximately)

5'-6"

⅛"-1'-0"
1"-1'-0"
Metric

Samuel Wilson, Jr., Del.

| U.S. DEPARTMENT OF THE INTERIOR OFFICE OF NATIONAL PARKS, BUILDINGS, AND RESERVATIONS BRANCH OF PLANS AND DESIGN | NAME OF STRUCTURE FRANK'S ISLAND LIGHTHOUSE NORTH-EAST PASS~MISSISSIPPI RIVER ~ PLAQUEMINES PARISH, LOUISIANA. JAN 31, 1935 | SURVEY NO. LA-19 | HISTORIC AMERICAN BUILDINGS SURVEY SHEET 1 OF 1 SHEETS | INDEX NO. |

1-055

1-055. Elevation and section, Frank's Island
Lighthouse, North East Pass, Mississippi
River, Louisiana. Samuel Wilson Jr., delin-
eator, 1935. P&P, HABS, LA,38-_____,1-.

Ocracoke Island Light, North Carolina

An early southern tower is located on Ocracoke Island, part of North Carolina's Outer Banks. It was built in 1823 by Noah Porter of Massachusetts. The tower is brick, stands 65 feet tall, and, rather unusually, remains as it was originally constructed.

1-056. Ocracoke Island Lighthouse, Ocracoke, North Carolina. 1936. AP, P&P, NYWTS, SUBJ/GEOG: LIGHTHOUSES–NORTH CAROLINA.

1-056

Owl's Head Light, Maine

One of Maine's numerous white conical towers, Owl's Head Light differs from the others in that it was built of brick rather than stone. It is one of a string of lighthouses that line the Penobscot Bay. Built in 1825, it stands 30 feet tall.

1-057

1-058

1-057. Owl's Head Lighthouse, Owl's Head, Maine. Richard Cheek, photographer, 1989. P&P, HABS, ME-185-3.

1-058. Lens and lantern, Owl's Head Lighthouse, Owl's Head, Maine. Richard Cheek, photographer, 1989. P&P, HABS, ME-185-3.

Dice Head (Old) Light, Maine

Put into service in 1829, Dice Head Light stands on the northern side of Penobscot Bay. It is a 51-foot-tall stone tower, although during much of its early life it was enclosed in wooden walls, which gave it the form of a hexagonal pyramid. A steel skeleton replaced it in 1937.

1-059. Dice Head Lighthouse with keeper's dwelling, shed, and oil house, Castine, Maine. Richard Cheek, photographer, 1990. P&P, HABS, ME-199-2.

1-059

1-060

1-061

1-060. Dice Head Lighthouse, Castine,
Maine. 1990. Richard Cheek, photographer,
1990. P&P, HABS, ME-199-6.

1-061. Iron stairway inside Dice Head
Lighthouse, Castine, Maine. Richard Cheek,
photographer, 1990. P&P, HABS, ME-199-7.

Fort Gratiot Lighthouse, Michigan

Fort Gratiot, named after Charles Gratiot, the engineer in charge of its construction and later Chief Engineer of the U.S. Army Corps of Engineers, was established in 1814 to guard the juncture of Lake Huron and the St. Clair River. A lighthouse originally built at the fort was replaced in 1829 by this lighthouse. (Lucius Lyon, its builder, later became one of Michigan's first U.S. senators.) It is a conical brick tower, painted white, and originally stood 65 feet tall. It was raised to 86 feet in the early 1860s.

1-062. Fort Gratiot Lighthouse, Port Huron, Michigan. Ca. 1900. DPCC, LC-D4-13255.

1-063. SS *Delaware* and Fort Gratiot Light, Port Huron, Michigan. Between 1900 and 1910. DPCC, LC-D4-70568.

1-062

1-063

Back River Lighthouse, Virginia

1-064. Back River Lighthouse, Hampton, Virginia. ACME photo, 1931. P&P, NYWTS, SUBJ/GEOG: LIGHTHOUSES–VIRGINIA.

Marking the entrance to the Back River in the vicinity of Hampton, Virginia, this small brick lighthouse was built offshore and connected to land by a long wooden footbridge. Lighted in 1829, it stood 30 feet tall on an 18-foot-diameter base that narrowed to 9 feet at the top. Decommissioned in 1936, it fell into ruin and eventually washed away.

1-064

Pemaquid Point Lighthouse, Maine

Standing on a point at the entrance to Muscongus Bay, the Pemaquid Point Lighthouse is another of Maine's white, conical towers. The 38-foot-tall stone tower went into service in 1835.

1-065

1-066

1-067

1-065. Pemaquid Point Lighthouse, Bristol, Maine. 1947. WC, P&P, SSF, LIGHTHOUSES—MAINE, PEMAQUID POINT LIGHT, MAINE.

1-066. Pemaquid Point Lighthouse, Bristol, Maine. 1989. Richard Cheek, photographer, 1989. P&P, HABS, ME-187-5.

1-067. Pemaquid Point Lighthouse looking up, Bristol, Maine. Richard Cheek, photographer, 1989. P&P, HABS, ME-187-7.

Eagle Island Lighthouse, Maine

1-068. Eagle Island Lighthouse, East Penobscot Bay, Maine. Joseph J. Kirkbride, photographer, 1884–1891. LC-USZ62-60611.

Another small stone tower on the Maine coast, the Eagle Island Lighthouse was built in 1838. Although only 30 feet tall, it stands on a high bluff and has a focal plane of 106 feet about the water.

1-068

Ned's Point Light, Massachusetts

Located at the entrance to Mattapoisett Harbor on Buzzard's Bay, this 39-foot-tall stone tower went into operation in 1838. It had stone cantilevered stairs.

1-069. Ned's Point Light, Mattapoisett, Massachusetts. Walter Payton, photographer, 1940. LC-USF33-015567-M2.

1-069

Dog Island Lighthouse, Florida

1-070. Dog Island Lighthouse, Dog Island, Florida. 1866. P&P, S, lot 13468.

1-071. Dog Island Lighthouse, Dog Island, Florida. Ca. 1866. P&P, S, lot 13468.

When a lighthouse was established on Dog Island (located off the Florida panhandle) in 1839, the keeper became the first known human inhabitant of the island. This 40-foot-tall tower was undermined by beach erosion and finally was destroyed by a hurricane about six years after these photographs were taken. The lighthouse was not rebuilt.

1-070

1-071

Southwest Pass Lighthouse, Louisiana

Built in 1840, this was the second lighthouse marking the entrance to the Southwest Pass through the Mississippi delta to the Mississippi River. But its site was too far from the entrance to the channel. When the tower fell victim to settlement and erosion, it was replaced by an iron skeleton tower (lighted in 1873, see 5-016).

1-072. Southwest Pass Lighthouse, Southwest Pass Entrance, Louisiana, 1867. P&P, S, lot 13458.

1-073. Views of the southwest pass of the Mississippi River [composite of three views: 1. southwest pass with pilot town in background; 2. lighthouse and west view of the pass; 3. pilot town], Louisiana. 1861. P&P, LC-USZ62-91425.

1-072

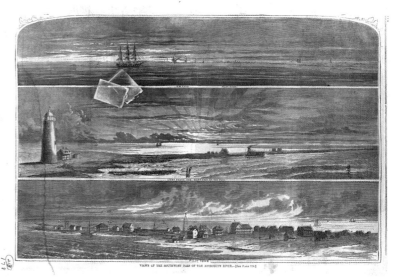

1-073

Cape Florida Lighthouse, Florida

1-074. Cape Florida Lighthouse, Key Biscayne, Florida. WC, P&P, LC-USZ62-74415.

1-075. Cape Florida Lighthouse, Key Biscayne, Florida. City of Miami News Bureau, 1952. P&P, NYWTS, SUBJ/GEOG: LIGHTHOUSES–CAPE FLORIDA–MIAMI, FLA.

Constructed to mark the entrance to the Biscayne Bay, the Cape Florida Lighthouse is brick and originally stood 65 feet tall. After being damaged in an Indian attack, it was rebuilt in 1846. However, the Light-House Board still considered it insufficiently tall. In 1855 it was raised to its present 95-foot height. It is painted white.

1-074

1-075

Sankaty Head Light, Massachusetts

This nearly cylindrical brick tower, located on the southeastern side of Nantucket Island, was lighted in 1850. It stands 70 feet tall and is painted with three bands—white on top and bottom, and red in the middle. The wooden keeper's dwelling seen in this picture is no longer standing.

1-076. Sankaty Head Lighthouse, Siasconset, Massachusetts. 1953. P&P, NYWTS, SUBJ/GEOG: LIGHTHOUSES– MASS-ACHUSETTS–NANTUCKET

1-076

Whitehead Island Light, Maine

1-077. Whitehead Island Lighthouse, Whitehead Island, Maine. Richard Cheek, photographer, 1991. P&P, HABS, ME-211-4.

1-078. Whitehead Island Lighthouse and keeper's dwelling, Whitehead Island, Maine. Richard Cheek, photographer, 1991. P&P, HABS, ME-211-2.

Located north of Monhegan Island Light, also at the entrance to the West Penobscot Bay, Whitehead Island Light (1852) is a 41-foot-tall granite tower that replaced an 1807 wooden pyramid. Because it resembles nearby Monhegan Island Light, designed by Alexander Parris and completed two years before, it may have been designed by Parris. Despite a general similarity, the two towers differ in their architectural details.

1-077

1-078

Alexander Parris's Lighthouses

Best known as architect of Quincy Market in Boston, Massachusetts, and other austere granite buildings in his native New England, Alexander Parris was also an engineer. In the late 1830s and 1840s he designed several lighthouses and beacons and even constructed a few of them himself. The lighthouses he built were at challenging sites and required a higher level of engineering expertise than did the usual towers.

His first executed project was Saddleback Ledge Lighthouse, built on a tiny island at the entrance to East Penobscot Bay in Maine. Competed in 1839, the lighthouse has walls of hammered stone and stands about 42 feet tall to the top of its lantern, with four levels inside in addition to the lantern. It measures 26 feet in diameter at the base and has an interior dimension of 19 feet. Originally the keeper and his family lived inside the tower; later a separate dwelling was added.

1-079. Site plan and location map, Saddleback Ledge Lighthouse, on Saddleback Ledge in Penobscot Bay, Maine. Robert Swilley, delineator, 1960. P&P, HABS, ME,7-ROCLA.V,1-, sheet no. 1.

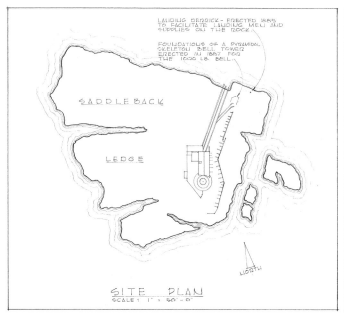

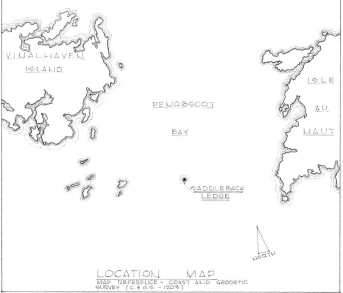

1-079

1-080. Second to fifth floor plans, Saddleback Ledge Lighthouse, on Saddleback Ledge in Penobscot Bay, Maine. Robert Swilley, delineator, 1960. P&P, HABS, ME,7-ROCLA.V,1-, sheet 3 of 3.

1-081. North side, Saddleback Ledge Lighthouse, on Saddleback Ledge in Penobscot Bay, Maine. Cervin Robinson, photographer, 1960. P&P, HABS, ME,7-ROCLA.V,1-1.

1-082. West side, Saddleback Ledge Lighthouse, on Saddleback Ledge in Penobscot Bay, Maine. Cervin Robinson, photographer, 1960. P&P, HABS, ME,7-ROCLA.V,1-2

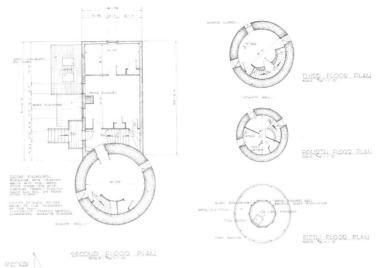

1-080

1-081

1-082

Matinicus Rock, 5 miles south of Matinicus Island in the entrance to Penobscot Bay, is another remote outcropping on the Maine coast. The first Matinicus Rock Lighthouse, a dwelling with towers at each end built in 1827, was damaged in a storm. The structure Parris designed to replace it also was a dwelling with towers at each end. This handsome, granite structure was completed in 1847. Ten years later, the light station was again rebuilt and the towers were more widely separated. Only the base of Parris's dwelling house remains. The surviving south tower, which dates from 1857, is a granite cylinder that stands 48 feet tall.

1-085. Matinicus Rock Lighthouse showing the twin towers of 1857, Matinicus Rock, Maine. W. Taber, 1897. Gen. Coll., *The Century: A Popular Quarterly* 54, no. 2 (June 1897).

1-086. Matinicus Rock Lighthouse, Matinicus Rock, Maine. Ca. 1893. Gen. Coll., *Annual Report of the Light-House Board*, 1894.

1-087. Light tower and keeper's dwelling with the abandoned lighthouse on the right, Matinicus Rock Lighthouse, Matinicus Rock, Maine. Richard Cheek, photographer, 1992. P&P, HABS, ME-210-1.

1-088. Keeper's dwelling and active light tower, Matinicus Rock Lighthouse, Matinicus Rock, Maine. Richard Cheek, photographer, 1992. P&P, HABS, ME-210-4.

1-085

1-086

1-088

1-087

Parris's Mount Desert Rock Lighthouse project also involved rebuilding a lighthouse on a remote Maine islet. Located over 20 miles from the nearest harbors on Mount Desert Island, Mount Desert Rock Lighthouse was considered the most isolated and exposed American lighthouse. Waves regularly swept over the rock. The first lighthouse there, built in 1830, was a cottage-style structure. Parris's granite tower, completed in 1848, resembled Saddleback Ledge except that it improved on the earlier structure in some details: both stood 42 feet to the underside of the gallery, but Mount Desert Rock Light had a wider diameter base (34 feet). Its height was raised in 1857, and it now stands 58 feet tall.

1-089. Mount Desert Rock Lighthouse, before a new dwelling was erected, south of Mount Desert Island, Maine. Ca. 1893. Gen. Coll., *Annual Report of the Light-House Board*, 1894.

1-090. Mount Desert Rock Lighthouse looking north, south of Mount Desert Island, Maine. Ca. 1893. Gen. Coll., *Annual Report of the Light-House Board*, 1894.

1-089

1-090

1-091. Mount Desert Rock Lighthouse, east (entrance) side, south of Mount Desert Island, Maine. Richard Cheek, photographer, 1990. P&P, HABS, ME-204-4.

1-092. Mount Desert Rock Lighthouse and keeper's dwelling, south of Mount Desert Island, Maine. Richard Cheek, photographer, 1990. P&P, HABS, ME-204-1.

1-091

1-092

Because it too was on a rocky outcropping, although in Long Island Sound, Execution Rocks Lighthouse was another project best handled by a skilled engineer. Parris designed this conical granite tower in collaboration with Grilley Bryant. First lighted in 1850, it stood 42 feet tall. After the Civil War, the tower was rebuilt: its height was increased to about 58 feet, and a separate granite dwelling was added to the station.

1-093. Execution Rocks Lighthouse, Long Island Sound, New York. C. E. Bolles, photographer, ca. 1896, P&P, LC-USZ62-115971.

1-093

1-094. Execution Rocks Lighthouse, Long Island Sound, New York. Ca. 1936. NYWTS, SUBJ/GEOG: LIGHTHOUSES–EXECUTION ROCK–LONG ISLAND SOUND.

1-095. Detail of tower, Execution Rocks Light Station, Long Island Sound, New York. Ca. 1936. NYWTS, SUBJ/GEOG: LIGHTHOUS-ES–EXECUTION ROCK–LONG ISLAND SOUND.

1-094

1-095

Less complicated structurally than the others were several granite towers in Maine in which Parris had a hand. One was Libby Island Light, located on an island at the entrance to the Machias Bay. This 42-foot-tall structure was completed in 1848. It originally had a spiral iron stairway and was lined with brick.

1-096. Libby Island Lighthouse, Libby Island, Machiasport, Maine. Richard Cheek, photographer, 1991. P&P, HABS, ME-218-3.

1-097. Iron stairway inside Libby Island Lighthouse, Libby Island, Machiasport, Maine. Richard Cheek, photographer, 1991. P&P, HABS, ME-218-4.

1-096

1-097

1-098. Monhegan Island Lighthouse, Monhegan Island, Maine. Richard Cheek, photographer, 1990. P&P, HABS, ME-202-6.

1-099. Monhegan Island Lighthouse and keeper's dwelling, Monhegan Island, Maine. Richard Cheek, photographer, 1990. P&P, HABS, ME-202-1.

Similar to Libby Island Light, Monhegan Island Light is a 47-foot-tall granite tower than replaced an earlier tower. It went into operation in 1850.

1-098

1-099

STONE AND

1 8 5 3 – 1 9 0 5

BRICK TOWERS

Although many new construction materials appeared in the second half of the nineteenth century, masonry continued to be a convenient and economical material for lighthouses. The most noteworthy development in this period with respect to masonry was the introduction of very tall towers.

In its 1852 report on the condition of lighthouses, the Light-House Board laid out a plan for a sequence of seacoast lights that would be visible from far out at sea. It determined that these lights should be 150 feet or more above sea level. The Board designated some existing towers to become seacoast lights, and it selected other locations for additional towers. The height of the existing towers had to be raised, and the new towers were built to unprecedented heights.

In a list of the lights needing to be raised, ranked in order of their importance, Cape Hatteras Lighthouse in North Carolina was at the top. The 1803 Cape Hatteras Lighthouse was raised to 150 feet above sea level in 1854, making it the first tall tower. Many other tall towers followed, including a new Cape Hatteras tower in 1870 that at nearly 200 feet above ground, was the tallest lighthouse in the world at the time (2-016–2-027). These tall towers were built of brick.

Absecon Light, New Jersey

Completed in 1857, the Absecon Lighthouse in Atlantic City, New Jersey, is an early tall tower. Built of brick in a slightly tapering form, it stands 169 feet tall. To make it more visible during the day, the tower was painted a light color with a darker band in the middle.

2-001

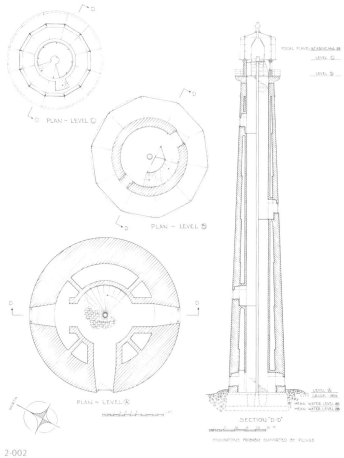

2-002

2-001. Absecon Lighthouse, Atlantic City, New Jersey. Ca. 1900. DPCC, LC-D4-5864.

2-002. Horizontal and vertical sections, Absecon Lighthouse, Atlantic City, New Jersey. John D. Milner, delineator, 1964. P&P, HABS, NJ,1-ATCI,2-.

Fire Island Lighthouse, New York

Among the towers the Light-House Board considered necessary to raise was Fire Island Lighthouse. A new tower (1858) replaced an earlier one. It has a somewhat flared base and stands 168 feet tall. Its distinctive markings are four bands, two black and two white.

2-003

2-004

2-003. The lighthouse keeper and his family at Fire Island Lighthouse, Long Island, New York. ACME Photo, 1934. NYWTS, SUBJ/GEOG: LIGHTHOUSES–FIRE ISLAND–N.Y.S.

2-004. Son of the lighthouse keeper on his way to school, Fire Island Lighthouse, Long Island, New York. Roger Higgins, photographer, 1952. NYWTS, SUBJ/GEOG: LIGHTHOUSES–FIRE ISLAND–N.Y.S.

Barnegat Lighthouse, New Jersey

This tall tower replaced the earlier Barnegat Lighthouse—a roughly 40-foot-tall tower that mariners found hard to make out, which met its end by toppling into the ocean. A site was selected south of the original tower, and the new tower was made a primary light. Constructed in 1857–1858 and first lighted on January 1, 1859, the tower was brick with a slender profile and stood 172 feet tall. Today its daymark colors are red on the top and white on the bottom. In 1933 a storm seriously eroded the beach on which it stood; steel shoring was put in to protect the lighthouse.

2-005. East elevation, Barnegat Lighthouse, Long Beach Island, New Jersey. Nathaniel R. Ewan, photographer, ca. 1920. P&P, HABS, NJ,15-BAR,1-1.

2-005

2-006

2-007

2-006. Barnegat Lighthouse, Long Beach Island, New Jersey. Velox Johnson Bros. Photo, 1925. NYWTS, SUBJ/GEOG: LIGHT-HOUSES–BARNEGAT LIGHT–BARNEGAT, NEW JERSEY.

2-007. Barnegat Lighthouse, Long Beach Island, New Jersey. After 1933. WC, P&P, SSF, LIGHTHOUSES—NEW JERSEY, BARNEGAT LIGHT.

Photo taken after steel shoring from Bethlehem Steel Company was placed to protect the base of the lighthouse.

Cape Lookout Lighthouse, North Carolina

Constructed between 1857 and 1859, this conical brick tower stood 150 feet tall. In 1872, to make it more effective as a daymark, the tower was painted in a bold black and white diamond pattern. It replaced a smaller lighthouse built in 1812.

2-008. Cape Lookout Lighthouse, Beaufort, North Carolina. P&P, SSF, LIGHTHOUSES—NORTH CAROLINA.

2-008

Cape May Point Lighthouse, New Jersey

2-009. Cape May Point Lighthouse, Cape May Point, New Jersey. Between 1900 and 1915. DPCC, LC-D4-39193.

Cape May Point Lighthouse, a conical brick tower, was completed in 1859 and stands 157 feet tall. It replaced two earlier towers on the site.

2-009

Pensacola Lighthouse, Florida

Lighted in 1859, like Cape May Point Lighthouse, Pensacola Lighthouse is a 160-foot-tall tower.

2-010

2-011

2-010. Pensacola Lighthouse and keeper's house, Pensacola, Florida. Jack E. Boucher, photographer, 1962. P&P, HABS, FLA,17-PENSA,6-1.

2-011. Top of Pensacola Lighthouse, Pensacola, Florida. Jack E. Boucher, photographer, 1974. P&P, HABS, FLA,17-PENSA,6-13.

2-012. Keeper's quarters, facing south,
Pensacola Lighthouse, Pensacola, Florida.
Jack E. Boucher, photographer, 1974. P&P,
HABS, FLA,17-PENSA,6-10.

2-013. Machinery for rotating the light,
Pensacola Lighthouse, Pensacola, Florida.
Jack E. Boucher, photographer, 1962. P&P,
HABS, FLA,17-PENSA,6-5.

2-014. Section and elevation, Pensacola
Lighthouse, Pensacola, Florida. John C.
Hecker, delineator, 1972. P&P, HABS,
FLA,17-PENSA,6-.

2-012

2-013

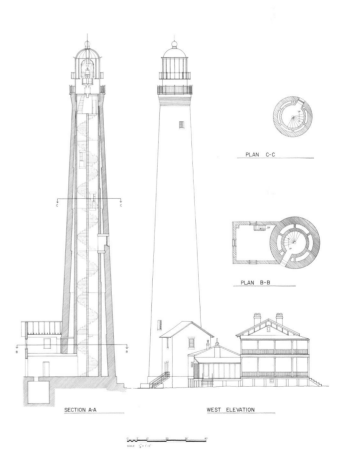

2-014

Assateague Island Lighthouse, Virginia

Work on this conical brick lighthouse started in 1860 but was suspended during the Civil War. The light was completed in 1867 and stands 142 feet tall. It is painted with red and white stripes. It replaced an earlier light.

2-015. Assateague Island Lighthouse, south end of Assateague Island, Virginia. P&P, SSF, LIGHTHOUSES—VIRGINIA.

2-015

Cape Hatteras Light, North Carolina

2-016. Decked out for the Coast Guard's 158th anniversary, Cape Hatteras Lighthouse, north of Cape Hatteras Point/Outer Banks, North Carolina. ACME Photo, 1948. NYWTS, SUBJ/GEOG: LIGHT-HOUSES–CAPE HATTERAS–NORTH CAROLI-NA.

Extending about 207 feet from the bottom of its underground foundation to its top, Cape Hatteras Light has the distinction of being the tallest American light tower. It is a conical brick structure on an octagonal, stone-trimmed base. The tower tapers upward from a diameter of about 32 1/2 feet above the base to about 17 feet under the lantern deck. Its spiral paint pattern makes it a memorable daymark. It was lighted in 1870.

The lighthouse was designed by engineers of the Fifth District of the Light-House Board and built with its own crew of mechanics. Baltimore manufacturers supplied bricks and metal work for the building. The first construction crew arrived at this remote site in November 1868 and built accommodations for themselves and facilities for their work, including a wharf and tram railroad to the building site. Then work on the tower began, progressing steadily, and in December 1870 the lens was installed.

Cape Hatteras Lighthouse continues to stand after being moved 2,900 feet in 1999 to a new site 1,600 feet inland from the Atlantic Ocean.

2-016

2-017

2-018

2-019

2-017. General view, Cape Hatteras Lighthouse at sunset looking west, north of Cape Hatteras Point/Outer Banks, North Carolina. John E. Boucher, photographer, 1989. P&P, HABS, NC,28-BUXT,1-6.

2-018. Front elevation, entry of Cape Hatteras Lighthouse, north of Cape Hatteras Point/Outer Banks, North Carolina. John E. Boucher, photographer, 1989. P&P, HABS, NC,28-BUXT,1-7.

2-019. Interior of base of tower showing iron stairway, weight well, and oil tank (top center), Cape Hatteras Lighthouse, north of Cape Hatteras Point/Outer Banks, North Carolina. John E. Boucher, photographer, 1989. P&P, HABS, NC,28-BUXT,1-15.

2-020. Interior view of the roof of the lantern (Fresnel lens has been removed), Cape Hatteras Lighthouse, north of Cape Hatteras Point/Outer Banks, North Carolina. John E. Boucher, photographer, 1989. P&P, HABS, NC,28-BUXT,1-25.

2-021. Iron gallery around the lantern room, Cape Hatteras Lighthouse, north of Cape Hatteras Point/Outer Banks, North Carolina. John E. Boucher, photographer, 1989. P&P, HABS, NC,28-BUXT,1-26.

2-022. Principal keeper's dwelling, Cape Hatteras Lighthouse, north of Cape Hatteras Point/Outer Banks, North Carolina. John E. Boucher, photographer, 1989. P&P, HABS, NC,28-BUXT,1-B-7.

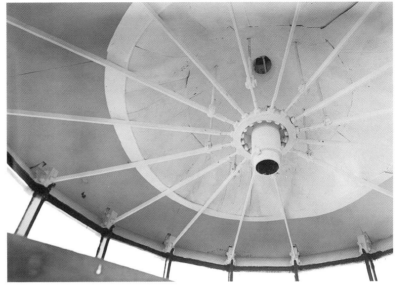

2-020

2-021

2-022

2-023

2-023. Double keeper's dwelling with principal keeper's dwelling on the right, Cape Hatteras Lighthouse, north of Cape Hatteras Point/Outer Banks, North Carolina. John E. Boucher, photographer, 1989. P&P, HABS, NC,28-BUXT,1-A-1.

2-024. Contemporary drawing, vertical section and front elevation, Cape Hatteras Lighthouse, north of Cape Hatteras Point/Outer Banks, North Carolina. Julius Bien, engraver, 1869. Gen. Coll., *Specifications for a Light-House to be Erected at Cape Hatteras, North Carolina* (Washington, DC: G.P.O., 1869).

2-025. Modern equivalent, section and east elevation, Cape Hatteras Lighthouse, north of Cape Hatteras Point/Outer Banks, North Carolina. Judith E. Collins, delineator, 1989. P&P, HABS, NC,28-BUXT,1-, sheet no. 2.

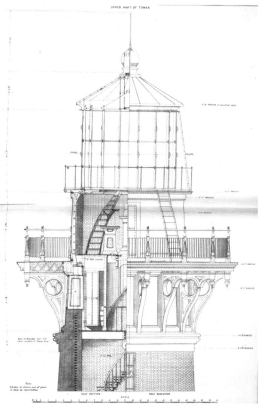

2-024

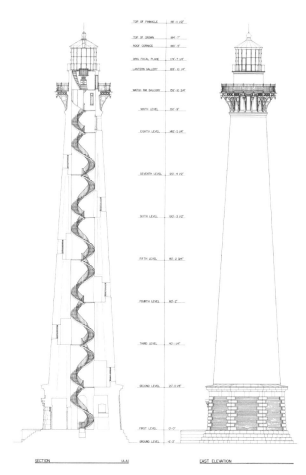

2-025

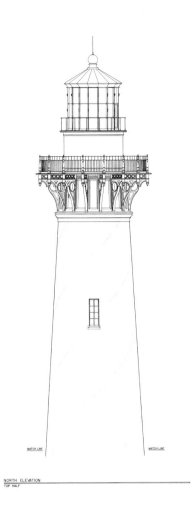

2-026

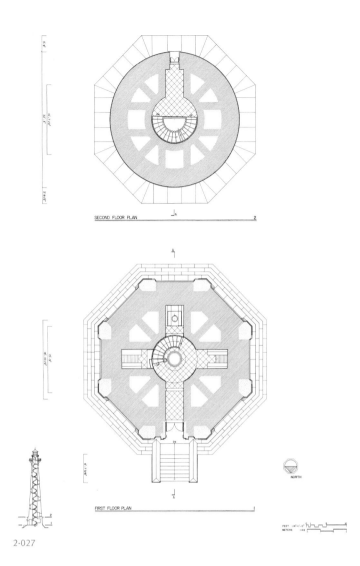

2-027

2-026. North elevation, top half of tower,
Cape Hatteras Light, north of Cape Hatteras
Point/Outer Banks, North Carolina. Judith E.
Collins, delineator, 1989. P&P, HABS,
NC,28-BUXT,1-, sheet no. 4.

2-027. First and second floor plans, Cape
Hatteras Light, north of Cape Hatteras
Point/Outer Banks, North Carolina. Judith E.
Collins, delineator, 1989. P&P, HABS,
NC,28-BUXT,1-, sheet no. 9.

Bodie Island Lighthouse, North Carolina

Another statuesque tower on the North Carolina Outer Banks, Bodie Island Lighthouse (1872) is a conical brick tower that stands 142 feet to the deck of the lantern. It rises from a granite pedestal and is painted with alternating light and dark bands. This lighthouse replaced two earlier towers, the second one having been destroyed by Confederate soldiers during the Civil War.

2-028

2-029

2-028. View of Bodie Island Lighthouse from the northeast, Outer Banks, near Nags Head, North Carolina. Jet Lowe, photographer, 2003. P&P, HABS, NC-395-49.

2-029. View of Bodie Island Lighthouse showing the keeper's dwelling, Outer Banks, near Nags Head, North Carolina. Jon A. Buono and James M. Womack, photographers, 2000–01. P&P, HABS, NC-395-2.

opposite
2-030. Bodie Island Lighthouse, Outer Banks, near Nags Head, North Carolina. Jon A. Buono and James M. Womack, photographers, 2000–01. P&P, HABS, NC-395-3.

2-031. Detail of brackets under gallery outside the lantern room, Bodie Island Lighthouse, Outer Banks, near Nags Head, North Carolina. Jet Lowe, photographer, 2003. P&P, HABS, NC-395-52.

2-032. Interior of Bodie Island Lighthouse looking up the iron spiral stairs, Outer Banks, near Nags Head, North Carolina. Jon A. Buono and James M. Womack, photographers, 2000–01. P&P, HABS, NC-395-20.

2-033. Inside the lantern room of Bodie Island Lighthouse showing the lens and glazing bars of the lantern, Outer Banks, near Nags Head, North Carolina. Jon A. Buono and James M. Womack, photographers, 2000–01. P&P, HABS, NC-395-23.

2-030

2-031

2-032

2-033

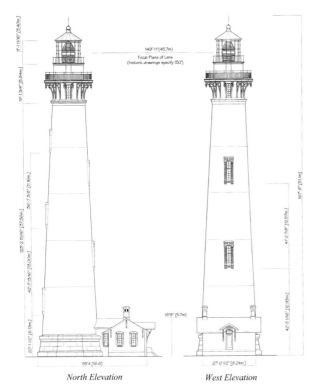

North Elevation   West Elevation

2-034

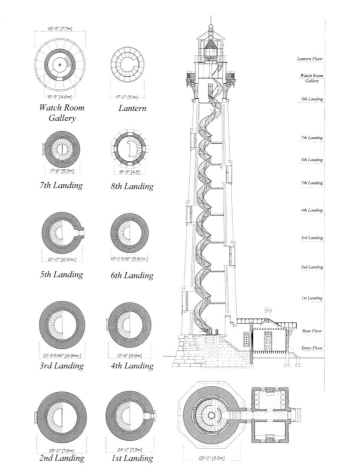

2-035

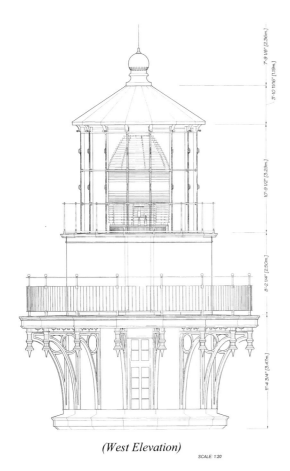

(West Elevation)

SCALE: 1:20

2-036

2-034. Bodie Island Lighthouse, tower elevations, Outer Banks, near Nags Head, North Carolina. Jared Benoit, Lisa Connor, and Todd Croteau, delineators. P&P, HABS, NC-395-, sheet no. 3.

2-035. Bodie Island Lighthouse, horizontal and vertical sections through the tower, Outer Banks, near Nags Head, North Carolina. Jared Benoit, Lisa Connor, and Todd Croteau, delineators, 2003. P&P, HABS, NC-395-, sheet no. 4.

2-036. Bodie Island Lighthouse, gallery and lantern elevation, Outer Banks, near Nags Head, North Carolina. Lisa Connor, delineator, 2003. P&P, HABS, NC-395-, sheet no.5.

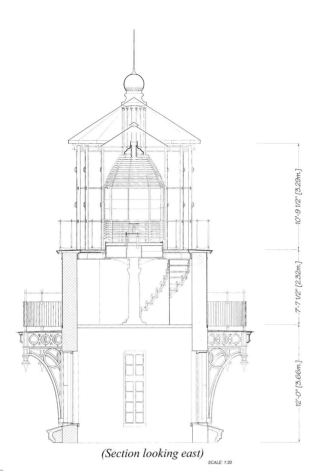

(Section looking east)

SCALE: 1:20

2-037

Note: Roof panels deleted to show framework

2 FEET

2-038

2-037. Bodie Island Lighthouse, gallery and lantern section, Outer Banks, near Nags Head, North Carolina. Lisa Connor, delineator, 2003. P&P, HABS, NC-395-, sheet no. 6.

2-038. Bodie Island Lighthouse, isometric view of lantern, Outer Banks, near Nags Head, North Carolina. Lisa Connor, delineator, 2003. P&P, HABS, NC-395-, sheet no. 7.

2-039. Bodie Island Lighthouse, cutaway view of lantern, Outer Banks, near Nags Head, North Carolina. Lisa Connor, delineator, 2003. P&P, HABS, NC-395-, sheet no. 8.

2-039

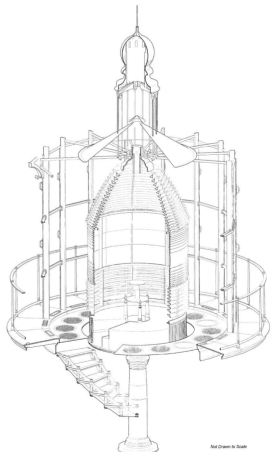

Not Drawn to Scale

St. Augustine Light, Florida

St. Augustine Lighthouse, located on Anastasia Island, is a conical brick tower, 165 feet tall, with black and white spiral marking. Constructed during the period 1871–1874, it replaced a Spanish watchtower that had been adapted for a lighthouse in the 1820s but was both too low and threatened by erosion. The site for the new tower was some distance from the old tower.

2-040. St. Augustine Lighthouse, Anastasia Island, Florida. Burgert Bros., photographer. P&P, LC-USZ62-73970.

2-041. St. Augustine Lighthouse, Anastasia Island, Florida. William Henry Jackson, photographer, ca. 1902. DPCC, LC-D4-14257.

2-041

2-040

2-042. Port Isabel (Point Isabel) Light, Brazos Santiago Pass, Texas. Arthur Rothstein, photographer, 1942. Farm Security Administration—Office of War Information Photograph Collection, LC-USF34-022069-D.

Port Isabel (Point Isabel) Light, Texas

Established in 1853, this conical brick tower stands 57 feet tall. Its top was raised in the 1880s to accommodate a new lens. It was deactivated in 1905.

2-042

2-043

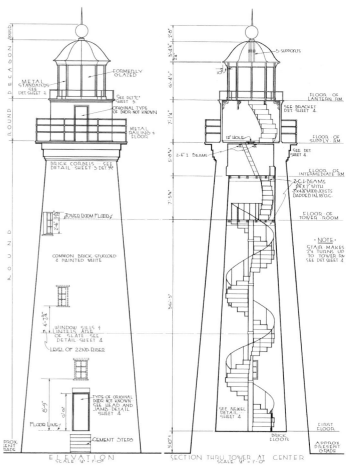

2-045

2-044

2-043. North elevation, Port Isabel (Point Isabel) Light, Brazos Santiago Pass, Texas. Bartlett Cocke, photographer, 1934. P&P, HABS, TEX,31-POISA,1-3.

2-044. Interior detail under the lantern floor, Port Isabel (Point Isabel) Light, Brazos Santiago Pass, Texas. Bartlett Cocke, photographer, 1934. P&P, HABS, TEX,31-POISA,1-5.

2-045. Elevation and section, Port Isabel (Point Isabel) Light, Brazos Santiago Pass, Texas. Zeb Rike, delineator, 1936. P&P, HABS, TEX,31-POISA,1-, sheet no. 2.

Boon Island Lighthouse, Maine

2-046. Plan and view of Boon Island Lighthouse, Boon Island, Maine. Brown and Hastings, delineators, 1850. Original in Records of U.S. Coast Guard, Record Group 26, National Archives, Washington, D.C. P&P, HABS, ME, 16-BOONI, 1-6.

Like many Maine lighthouses, Boon Island Light is built on a rock outcropping, with only about a half acre exposed at high water, roughly 6 1/2 miles from the nearest land. The first aid to navigation placed on the island was a wooden octagon 40 feet tall, but a storm soon swept it away. Another unlighted beacon replaced it. The first lighthouse on the island, completed in 1811, was demolished in an 1831 gale. A taller tower followed, but it was considered insufficiently tall by mid-century.

At the request of the Treasury Department, Gridley Bryant, an important Boston engineer, inventor, and building contractor, surveyed the lighthouse site in 1850. His plan and elevation (2-046) shows existing conditions at the site, including the second lighthouse, keeper's quarters, and outbuildings. Bryant worked on several light stations in Maine, usually in collaboration with Alexander Parris (see 1-079–1-099). In 1847 he built a boat slip on Boon Island.

The third tower was lighted on January 1, 1855. It is granite, like its predecessor, but very tall and slender. The tower stands 118 feet tall and measures 20 feet in diameter above its slightly flared base (25 feet in diameter); the structure tapers to 12 1/2 feet in diameter at the top. It is similar to the contemporaneous lighthouse on Petit Manan Island (2-051). Both towers are the tallest in New England.

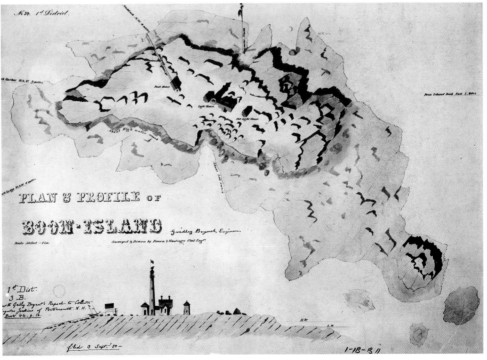

2-046

2-047

2-047. View of Boon Island Lighthouse from the air, Boon Island, Maine. First Coast Guard District Office, Boston, Massachusetts, ca. 1950. P&P, HABS, ME,16-BOONI,1-1.

2-048. Boon Island Lighthouse, Boon Island, Maine. First Coast Guard District Office, Boston, Massachusetts, 1946. P&P, HABS, ME,16-BOONI,1-2.

2-049. Boon Island Lighthouse, Boon Island, Maine. Between 1905 and 1920. DPCC, LC-D4-36897.

2-050. Oil house and bell, Boon Island Lighthouse, Boon Island, Maine. First Coast Guard District Office, Boston, Massachusetts. P&P, HABS, ME,16-BOONI,1-4.

2-048

2-049

2-050

Petit Manan Island Light, Maine

Located on a small island in the Gulf of Maine, Petit Manan Island Light replaced an 1817 lighthouse. It went into service in 1855, the same year as the structurally similar Boon Island Light. Both are slender conical towers, about the same height, and made of smooth granite. Petit Manan lacks the flared base of Boon Island.

2-051. Petit Manan Lighthouse, Petit Manan Island, Maine. Richard Cheek, photographer, 1990. P&P, HABS, ME-194-4.

2-051

Cockspur Island Light, Georgia

Replacing an earlier lighthouse, this brick tower was completed in 1857. It stands 46 feet tall.

2-052

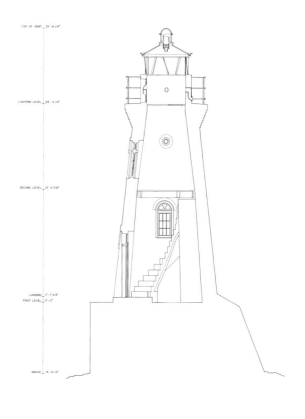

2-053

2-052. West elevation, Cockspur Island Light, Georgia. Judith E. Collins, photographer, 1994. P&P, HABS, GA,26-SAV.V,4-4.

2-053. Section through Cockspur Island Light, Georgia. Judith E. Collins, delineator, 1994. P&P, HABS, GA,26-SAV.V,4-.

Minnesota Point Lighthouse, Minnesota

Completed in 1858, this conical tower marked the Superior Entry in the sandbar that gave access from Lake Superior to the ports of Duluth and Superior. It was discontinued in 1885; only ruins remain.

2-054

2-055

2-054. Minnesota Point Lighthouse, near Duluth, Minnesota. L. P. Gallagher, photographer, 1934, from an old photograph. P&P, HABS, MINN,69-DULU,4-.

2-055. View of the ruins of Minnesota Point Lighthouse from the northwest, near Duluth, Minnesota. L. P. Gallagher, photographer, 1934. P&P, HABS, MINN,69-DULU, 4-1.

West Quoddy Head Lighthouse, Maine

2-056. West Quoddy Head Lighthouse and keeper's dwelling, Lubec, Maine. Richard Cheek, photographer, 1992. P&P, HABS, ME-208-3.

Unlike its demure, whitewashed cousins along the Maine coast, the West Quoddy Head Light sports a festive, peppermint-striped paintjob. Built in 1858 and standing 49 feet tall, it marks Quoddy Narrows between the United States and Canada.

2-056

Wood Island Lighthouse, Maine

Standing on Wood Island, off Biddeford Pool at the mouth of the Saco River, Wood Island Lighthouse (1858) is a conical granite structure that stands 47 feet tall.

2-057

2-058

2-057. Wood Island Lighthouse, Wood Island, Maine. Richard Cheek, photographer, 1991. P&P, HABS, ME-222-3.

2-058. Wood Island Lighthouse and keeper's dwelling, Wood Island, Maine. Richard Cheek, photographer, 1991. P&P, HABS, ME-222-1.

Cape San Blas Lighthouse, Florida

2-059. Cape San Blas Lighthouse, near Apalachicola, Florida. 1866. P&P, S, lot 13468.

The third Cape San Blas Lighthouse was completed in 1859. Its site became so eroded that the tower ultimately stood in the water, which caused it to topple over in 1882.

2-059

Jupiter Inlet Light, Florida

Put into operation in 1860, this brick tower stands 105 feet tall.

2-060. Jupiter Inlet Light, Jupiter, Florida. William Henry Jackson, photographer, between 1880 and 1897. DPCC, LC-D4-3671.

2-061. Jupiter Inlet Light from across the water, Jupiter, Florida. William Henry Jackson, photographer, between 1880 and 1897. DPCC, LC-D418-8038.

2-060

2-061

Thacher's Island (Cape Ann) Lights, Massachusetts

2-062. Thacher's Island (Cape Ann) Lights, south tower, Cape Ann, Massachusetts. Hervey Friend, photographer, ca. 1869. P&P, S, lot 13505.

2-063. Thacher's Island (Cape Ann) Lights, north tower, Cape Ann, Massachusetts. Hervey Friend, photographer, ca. 1869. P&P, S, lot 13505.

The twin lights at Thacher's Island, also called the Cape Ann Lights, are conical granite towers, lighted in 1861. They replaced a light station that was established at this place before the Revolutionary War. Both towers were 124 feet tall.

2-062

2-063

Isle of Shoals (White Island) Light, New Hampshire

This granite tower, lighted in 1865, stands 58 feet tall.

2-064. Isle of Shoals (White Island) Lighthouse, White Island, New Hampshire. H. G. Peabody, photographer, Ca. 1888. P&P, LC-USZ62-89697.

2-065. Isle of Shoals (White Island) Lighthouse, White Island, New York. Ca. 1901. DPCC, LC-D4-13923.

2-064

2-065

St. Marks Lighthouse, Florida

St. Marks Lighthouse was constructed after the Civil War with the bricks of an earlier tower that the Confederates damaged during the war. Standing 73 feet tall, the rebuilt tower was lighted in 1867. Today it is the rear part of St. Marks Range Lights.

2-066

Erie Land (Old Presque Isle) Light, Pennsylvania

Lighted in 1867, as noted on the stone over the entry, this sandstone tower replaced the original 1819 light at Erie, which was the first American light on the Great Lakes. The tower measured 49 feet tall and had slightly tapering walls, inclining from 19 feet in diameter at the base to 14 feet at the top. It lacked a lantern when the Historic American Building Survey (HABS) recorded it in 1936, but the lantern was restored in 1990.

2-067. West side, Erie Land (Old Presque Isle) Light, Erie, Pennsylvania. William J. Bulger, photographer, 1936. P&P, HABS, PA,25-ERI,5-1.

2-068. Main entrance (west side), Erie Land (Old Presque Isle) Light, Erie, Pennsylvania. William J. Bulger, photographer, 1936. P&P, HABS, PA,25-ERI,5-3.

2-067

2-068

Presque Island Lighthouse, Michigan

2-069. Presque Island Lighthouse, Presque Isle Peninsula/Lake Huron, Michigan. WC, P&P, SSF, LIGHTHOUSES—MICHIGAN, PRESQUE ISLE.

Put into service in 1871, this lighthouse is a conical brick tower that stands 109 feet tall. It is painted white.

2-069

Pigeon Point Lighthouse, California

This classic-looking tower is unusual for California: with its high bluffs, the California coastline offers many elevated sites for lighthouses, making tall towers unnecessary. The 115-foot-tall Pigeon Point Lighthouse, near Pescadero, is a brick tower, painted white. It was lighted in 1872.

2-070. General view from the north, Pigeon Point Lighthouse, near Pescadero, California. Arthur Spaulding Co., photographer, 1928. P&P, HABS, CAL,41-PESC.V,1-19.

2-070

2-071

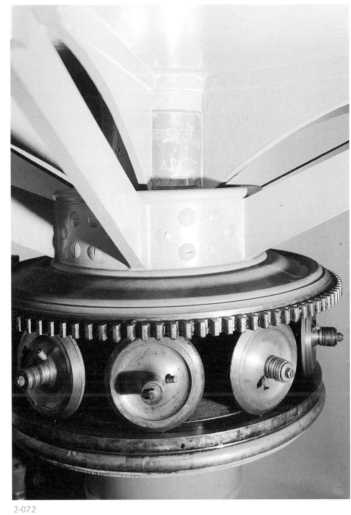

2-072

2-071. Lighthouse tower and watch house from east, Pigeon Point Lighthouse, near Pescadero, CA. Jack E. Boucher, photographer, 1975. P&P, HABS, CAL,41-PESC.V,1-3.

2-072. Detail of rotating mechanism at base of lantern with a brass plate that reads, "Henry Lepaute À Paris," Pigeon Point Lighthouse, near Pescadero, California. Jack E. Boucher, photographer, 1975. P&P, HABS, CAL,41-PESC.V,1-16.

2-073. Elevation and plan, Pigeon Point Lighthouse, near Pescadero, California. Amy Weinstein, delineator, 1974. P&P, HABS, CAL,41-PESC.V,1-.

GALLERY AND WATCH ROOM

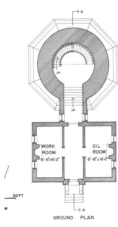

WORK ROOM
8'-6"x16'-2"

OIL ROOM
8'-8" x 16'-2"

20 FT

GROUND PLAN

2-073

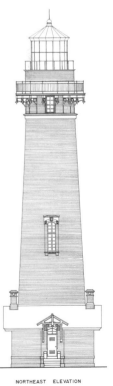

NORTHEAST ELEVATION

South Manitou Island Light, Michigan

South Manitou Island Light, a 65-foot-tall brick tower, went into operation in 1872, although a plaque over the entry says 1871. The structure has double walls with an air space between. It replaced a cottage-style lighthouse built in 1858; this was converted into a dwelling, which was then attached to the new tower by a covered walkway.

2-074. South Manitou Island Light, Glen Arbor, Michigan. John McWilliams, photographer, 1990. P&P, HABS, MICH,45-GLAR,8-.

2-074

2-075. View of the south (front) side, South Manitou Island Light, Glen Arbor, Michigan. John McWilliams, photographer, 1990. P&P, HABS, MICH,45-GLAR,8A-4.

2-076. Stairway in the lighthouse, South Manitou Island Light, Glen Arbor, Michigan. John McWilliams, photographer, 1990. P&P, HABS, MICH,45-GLAR,8A-7.

2-077. Dwelling of South Manitou Island Light completed 1858, Glen Arbor, Michigan. John McWilliams, photographer, 1990. P&P, HABS, MICH,45-GLAR,8A-6.

2-075

2-076

2-077

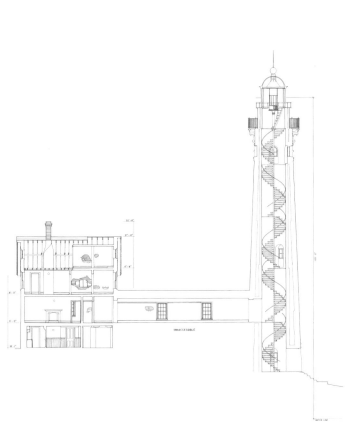

2-078

2-079

2-080

2-078. Section through South Manitou Island Lighthouse and dwelling, Glen Arbor, Michigan. Judith Collins, delineator, 1988. P&P, HABS, MICH,45-GLAR,8A-.

2-079. Oil storage shed, South Manitou Island Light, Glen Arbor, Michigan. John McWilliams, photographer, 1990. P&P, HABS, MICH,45-GLAR,8B-1.

2-080. Fog signal building, South Manitou Island, Glen Arbor, Michigan. John McWilliams, photographer, 1990. P&P, HABS, MICH,45-GLAR,8C-.

Ponquogue/Shinnecock Lighthouse, New York

2-081. Ponquogue/Shinnecock Lighthouse, Long Island, New York. U.S. Coast Guard, 1948. NYWTS, SUBJ/GEOG: LIGHTHOUSES–PONQUOQUE LIGHT–LONG ISLAND, NY.

After the Coast Guard replaced this structure, it wanted the lighthouse site for other purposes. So, in 1948, the lighthouse was demolished. The photograph documents its destruction.

2-081

Among the most dramatic and technically accomplished lighthouses are those built on rocks and shoals projecting from the water or on water-covered sites. The pioneering example of an off-shore "sea-rock" lighthouse is the Eddystone Lighthouse. Marking Eddystone Rocks in the English channel south of the important port of Plymouth, the first Eddystone Lighthouse was constructed during the period 1696–1699. The fourth tower was built during the period 1878–1882 (see 1-002). This and Bell Rock Lighthouse (1811; see 1-1003) served as models and inspiration for American sea-rock lighthouses.

Minot's Ledge Lighthouse, Massachusetts

Arguably the greatest achievement in American lighthouse engineering, Minot's Ledge Light was built on a rock that was usually covered with water. It was the second lighthouse on the site, which marked a dangerous ledge located over a mile from the Massachusetts coast. The conical granite tower stood 114 feet tall. The first 40 feet of the structure was entirely solid, made of dowelled and interlocking granite blocks; the open upper section served as bedrooms and a kitchen for the keepers who lived at the light when on duty. Construction took place between 1855 and 1860. The stone was cut and preassembled on land, then shipped out to the lighthouse site. It replaced an iron skeleton lighthouse that collapsed in 1851 (see 5-003 and 5-004).

2-082

2-082. Minot's Ledge Lighthouse in calm seas, near Cohasset, Massachusetts. Between 1880 and 1899. DPCC, LC-D4-3098 C.

2-083. Elevation, section, and plans of Minot's Ledge Lighthouse, near Cohasset, Massachusetts. E. Burrill, delineator, 1860. P&P, LC-USZ62-2481.

This drawing shows an elevation and section through the lighthouse and plans of successive levels of the structure.

2-084. "Setting the masonry on Government Island," preparing to build Minot's Ledge Lighthouse, near Cohasset, Massachusetts. 1896. Gen. Coll., *New England Magazine* 15 (October 1896): 136.

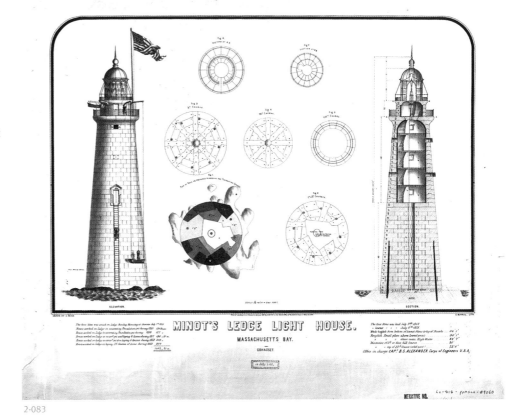

2-083

2-084

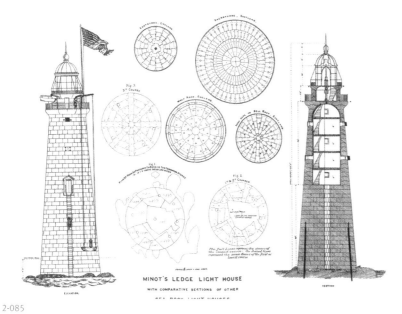

MINOT'S LEDGE LIGHT HOUSE
WITH COMPARATIVE SECTIONS OF OTHER

2-085

2-085. Elevation drawing from the 1893 Columbian Exposition of Minot's Lighthouse, near Cohasset, Massachusetts. Ca. 1893. Gen. Coll., *Annual Report of the Light-House Board*, 1894.

2-086. Waves surge against the base of Minot's Ledge Lighthouse in a storm, near Cohasset, Massachusetts. 1941. AP, P&P, NYWTS, SUBJ/GEOG: LIGHTHOUSES–MINOT'S LIGHT–BOSTON, MASS.

2-087. Waves surge against the base of Minot's Ledge Lighthouse in a storm, near Cohasset, Massachusetts. 1941. AP, P&P, NYWTS, SUBJ/GEOG: LIGHTHOUSES–MINOT'S LIGHT–BOSTON, MASS.

2-086

2-087

Whaleback Ledge Light, Maine

2-088. Whaleback Ledge Lighthouse, near Kittery Point, Maine. Ca. 1900. DPCC, LC-D4-13928.

2-089. Whaleback Ledge Lighthouse, near Kittery Point, Maine. Ca. 1900. DPCC, LC-D4-13928.

The entrance to the harbor of Portsmouth, New Hampshire, is marked by a lighthouse standing on a small outcropping called Whale's Back or Whaleback Ledge. Although the site was not as exposed as Minot's Ledge, it too was frequently submerged and regularly battered by heavy seas. To elevate the lighthouse, a stone platform 48 feet in diameter was built on the ledge. The tower, completed in 1831, was stone and conical in shape. The lighthouse was the subject of several inspections in the early nineteenth century, because of concerns that the structure was deteriorating. Nevertheless it stood until 1869, undergoing only occasional repairs at that time, Congress authorized funds for a new lighthouse. Lighted in 1872, the new structure was made of dovetailed granite blocks and resembled its predecessor in shape and height.

The structure on the left is the remains of the early tower, which served as the base for an iron fog signal building. The new tower (right) went up next to the old one. The fog structure is no longer standing.

2-088

2-089

Spectacle Reef Lighthouse, Michigan

Spectacle Reef Lighthouse is located at the northern end of Lake Huron near the Straights of Mackinac. Lighted in 1874, the structure was built on a reef covered with about 11 feet of water, 10 1/2 miles from shore. Construction began by building a square timber crib, 92 feet per side and 24 feet tall, with an interior well measuring 48 feet in diameter that was to hold a cofferdam (a temporary dam used to keep water out of an underwater construction area). The crib was towed to the site and filled with stones to sink it in place. Inside this frame, a cylindrical wooden cofferdam—like a huge barrel—was placed, made watertight, and pumped out. Construction of the lighthouse took place inside the cofferdam: the surface of the reef was prepared and the first courses of the stone tower were constructed. When complete, the conical limestone tower stood 80 feet above the rock, tapering from a 32-foot-diameter base to 18 feet at the cornice. The tower is solid for 34 feet above the base — composed of interlocking blocks like those in its model, Minot's Ledge Lighthouse (2-082–2-087) — and similarly bolted to the ground and to each other.

2-090. Vertical section and plan of courses of stone base, Spectacle Reef Lighthouse, Lake Huron, Michigan. Ca. 1893. Gen. Coll., *Annual Report of the Light-House Board*, 1894.

2-091. Spectacle Reef Lighthouse in winter, Lake Huron, Michigan. 1874. Gen. Coll., "The Light-Houses of the United States," *Harper's New Monthly Magazine* (March 1874): 471.

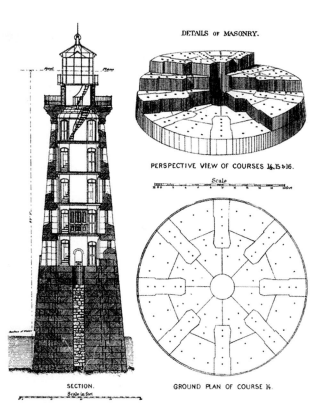

DETAILS OF MASONRY.

PERSPECTIVE VIEW OF COURSES 14, 15 & 16.

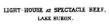
Scale

SECTION.
Scale in feet

GROUND PLAN OF COURSE 14.

LIGHT-HOUSE AT SPECTACLE REEF,
LAKE HURON.

2-090

2-091

Tillamook Rock Lighthouse, Oregon

The site chosen for this lighthouse was an islet located about a mile seaward from Tillamook Head on the Oregon coast, about 20 miles south of the entrance to the Columbia River. It was a desolate location, the nearest harbor at the time being about 20 miles away. Even landing a boat at the rock proved nearly impossible. The project began inauspiciously in 1879 with the drowning death of the masonry foreman at the site. Because of the difficulty in landing, a cable was rigged between the rock and a supply steamer moored nearby; men and supplies were hauled to and from the rock across the cable. Later, steam-powered boom-derricks were constructed on the rock; their long booms made landing the construction materials somewhat easier. Ladder-derricks at the site helped masons raise the stones. The irregular surface of the rock had to be blasted and drilled to create level surfaces for the lighthouse and other structures.

The lighthouse consisted of a stone tower, 16 feet square, that rose from the center of the dwelling, also of stone. The dwelling was one story tall, measuring 48 by 45 feet, with an extension on one side for a fog siren structure. The dwelling was designed to accommodate four keepers and a six-months' supply of provisions and coal. The lighthouse went into operation in 1881.

2-092. Tillamook Rock Lighthouse under construction, showing sea at the lowest stage and quiet, off Tillamook Head, Oregon. R. M. Tabor, delineator, ca. 1881. Gen. Coll., *Annual Report of the Light-House Board*, 1881.

2-092

2-093. Tillamook Rock Lighthouse completed, view in rough southerly sea, off Tillamook Head, Oregon. R. M. Tabor, delineator, ca. 1881. Gen. Coll., *Annual Report of the Light-House Board*, 1881.

2-094. Tillamook Rock and Lighthouse, off Tillamook Head, Oregon. S. B. Crow, photographer, 1891. P&P, SSF, LIGHTHOUSES —OREGON.

2-095. Tillamook Rock Lighthouse, off Tillamook Head, Oregon. ACME Photo, 1940. P&P, NYWTS, SUBJ/GEOG: LIGHTHOUSES —GENERAL.

2-093

2-094

2-095

St. George's Reef Lighthouse, California

Work at this islet began after Tillamook Rock Lighthouse had been completed, so its engineers were able to learn from that earlier experience. This lighthouse also is on the Pacific Coast, off the northern coast of California. Here too the cable system for landing materials was used during the early days of construction, in 1883. Work was suspended for a period, then resumed in 1887 and continued for the next four years. Lighted in 1892, the lighthouse is a square, pyramidal building 90 feet tall and made of granite.

2-096. St. George's Reef Lighthouse, near Crescent City, California. 1884. Gen. Coll., *Annual Report of the Light-House Board*, 1884.

St. George's Reef Lighthouse, built on Northwest Seal Rock, showing the rock at the close of the working 1884 season and the method of landing men from the schooner *La Ninfa*.

ST. GEORGE'S REEF LIGHT STATION.
View from the South-West, showing the Rock as it appeared at the End of the Working Season, and the Method of Landing Men from the Schooner "La Ninfa".

2-096

Graves Lighthouse, Massachusetts

Despite its ominous name, Graves Ledge was named for a naval officer, not for the number of vessels it wrecked. It is located at the outer edge of Boston Harbor, near Broad Sound Channel, a shipping channel that was opened in the early twentieth century. Put into operation in 1905, Graves Lighthouse is a conical granite structure that stands 113 feet tall. The keepers lived inside the lighthouse.

2-097

2-098

ATTACHED TOWER AND HOUSE

These independent towers were connected to the keeper's house, usually with a covered walkway so the keeper did not have to go outside to reach the lantern. In the 1870s, under architect Paul Pelz (2-105–2-127), these individual parts were integrated through the design, resulting in some of the nation's architecturally finest lighthouses.

Rock Harbor Lighthouse, Michigan

Established in 1855 on Lake Superior, this nearly cylindrical tower was made of brick and stone and stood 50 feet tall.

2-099. View of west (front) side, Rock Harbor Lighthouse, Copper Harbor Vic., Michigan. Jack E. Boucher, photographer, 1961. P&P, HABS, MICH,42-COPHAR.V,2-3.

2-099

2-100. Rock Harbor Lighthouse, Copper Harbor Vic. Michigan. Jack E. Boucher, photographer, 1961. P&P, HABS, MICH,42-COPHAR.V,2-1.

2-101. South and east elevations, Rock Harbor Lighthouse, Copper Harbor Vic. Michigan. David E. Naill and Michael A. Kraeling, delineators, 1992. P&P, HABS, MICH,42-COPHAR.V,2-.

2-100

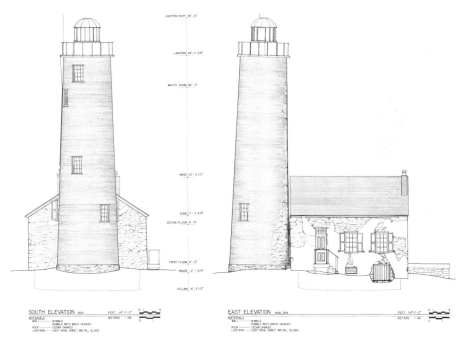

2-101

Michigan Island Lighthouse, Wisconsin

Michigan Island Lighthouse, lighted in 1857, is a conical tower standing 64 feet tall. It is made of stone, stuccoed and painted white, and attached to a one-and-a-half-story house. The lighthouse was not built in the originally planned location and therefore was discontinued until 1869, when it was lighted again. Although it was replaced in 1929, the lighthouse was allowed to remain standing.

2-102. Elevation, Michigan Island Lighthouse, Apostle Islands/Lake Superior, Wisconsin. Eva H. Kunckel and Daniel J. Lind, delineators, 1990. P&P, HABS, WIS,2-LPOIT.V,3A-, sheet no 2.

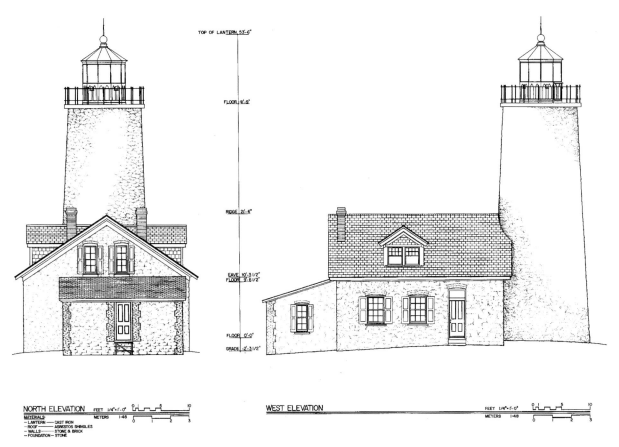

NORTH ELEVATION FEET 1/4"=1'-0"

MATERIALS:
- LANTERN ── CAST IRON
- ROOF ── ASBESTOS SHINGLES
- WALLS ── STONE & BRICK
- FOUNDATION ── STONE

WEST ELEVATION FEET 1/4"=1'-0"

2-102

2-103. Elevation and section, Michigan Island Lighthouse, Apostle Islands/Lake Superior, Wisconsin. Anne S. Beckett, delineator, 1990. P&P, HABS, WIS,2-LPOIT.V,3A-, sheet no. 3.

2-104. First and second floor plans, Michigan Island Light Station, Apostle Islands/Lake Superior, Wisconsin. Eva H. Kunckel, delineator, 1990. P&P, HABS, WIS,2-LPOIT.V,3A-, sheet no. 1.

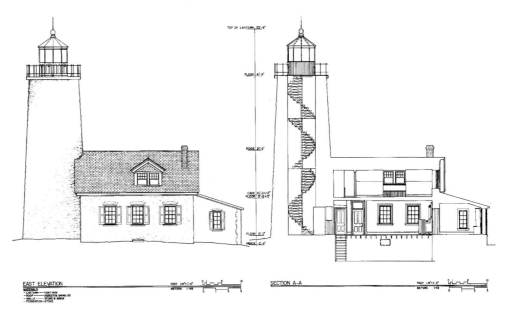

2-103

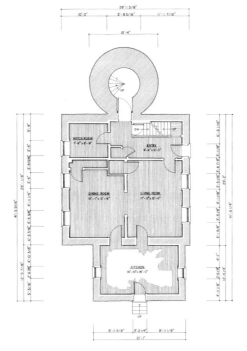

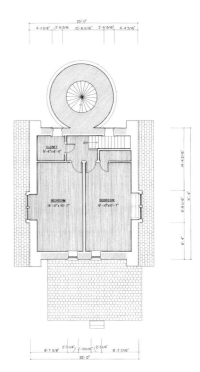

2-104

Lighthouses Built under Paul Pelz

A number of architecturally distinguished connected towers and houses were erected during the 1870s, the period when architect Paul Johannes Pelz worked as chief drafts-man for the Light-House Board. Educated in his native Germany, he trained in architecture in the office of a New York architect. Pelz's most important architectural project was the 1892 design for the new Library of Congress.

Around 1865 he began working as a draftsman with the Light-House Board, and between 1872 and 1877 he served as the Board's chief draftsman. During this period, lighthouses were designed with greater concern for their aesthetic effect. This is especially evident in the towers attached to houses, which were treated as a unit rather than as two structures and were unified through materials and ornamentation (see also 4-015 and 5-027).

Although architecturally reserved, the Presque Isle Lighthouse in Erie, Pennsylvania, has been treated as a unit. A brick dwelling with an attached tower, it went into service in 1873. The square tower stands 68 feet tall.

2-105. North elevation, Presque Isle Lighthouse, Erie, Pennsylvania. W. H. Adams and J. B. Evans, delineators, 1962. P&P, HABS, PA,25-ERI,8-, sheet no. 4.

The top portion of the tower is detached and placed on the right due to size constraints of the drawing.

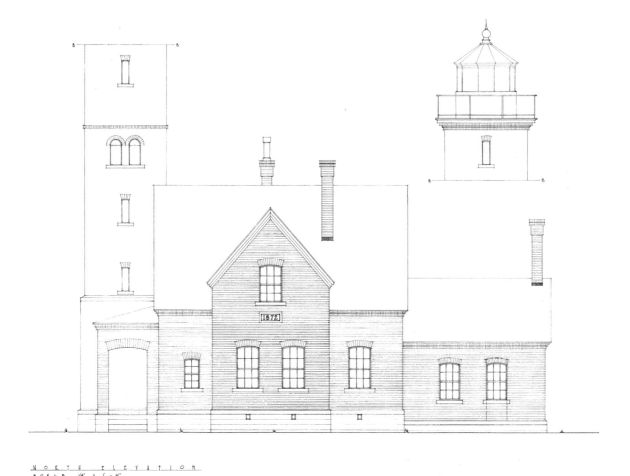

NORTH ELEVATION
SCALE ¼" = 1'-0"

2-105

2-106. Elevation, Presque Isle Lighthouse, Erie, Pennsylvania. W. H. Adams and J. B. Evans, delineators, 1962. P&P, HABS, PA,25-ERI,8-, sheet no. 5.

Here again, the top portion of the tower is detached and placed on the left due to size constraints of the drawing.

2-107. First floor plan, Presque Isle Lighthouse, Erie, Pennsylvania. W. H. Adams and J. B. Evans, delineators, 1962. P&P, HABS, PA,25-ERI,8-, sheet no. 1.

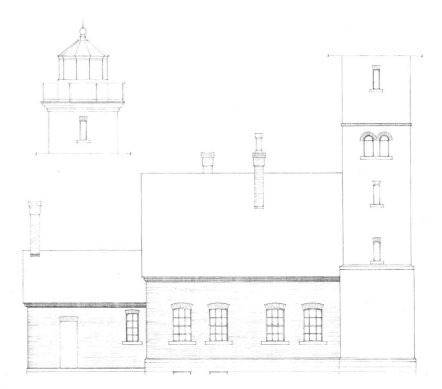

2-106

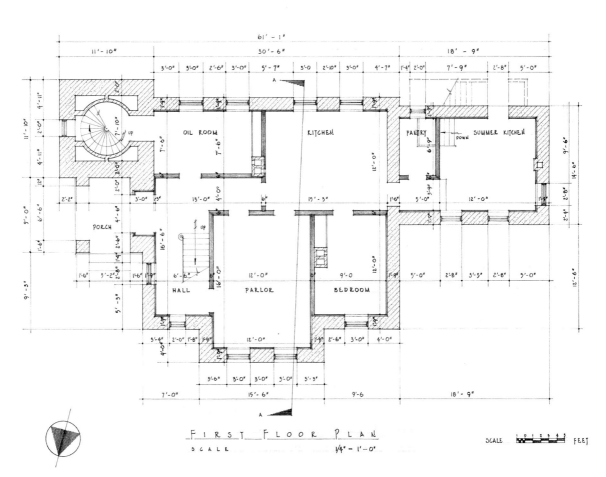

2-107

The Cleveland Lighthouse, an ornate brick tower and dwelling, was located at Main and Water Streets in Cleveland, Ohio. It was lighted in 1873 and operated for just nineteen years, at which point it was judged unnecessary.

2-108. Cleveland Lighthouse, Cleveland, Ohio. 1872. Gen. Coll., *Annual Report of the Light-House Board*, 1872.

2-108

2-109. Elevation, Au Sable Light Station, southern shore of Lake Superior, Grand Marais Vic., Michigan. Hugh Hughes, delineator, 1988. P&P, HABS, MICH,2-GRAMA.V,1-.

Two lighthouses on Lake Superior, Au Sable Lighthouse in Michigan and Outer Island Lighthouse in Wisconsin, are architecturally similar. Both are handsome brick towers attached to two-story brick houses. The Au Sable Lighthouse, lighted in 1874, stands 87 feet tall.

The Outer Island Lighthouse, also established in 1874, at 90 feet is a little taller than its architecturally similar neighbor.

SOUTH ELEVATION

FEET ¼"=1'-0"   0 1 2 3 4 5   10
METERS 1:48   0   1   2   3

2-109

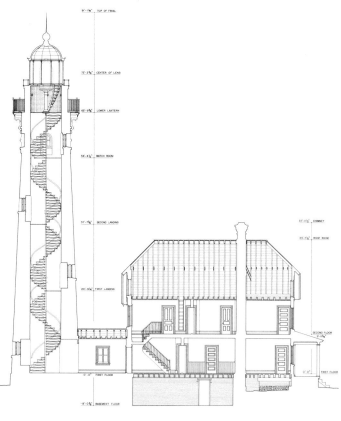

2-110

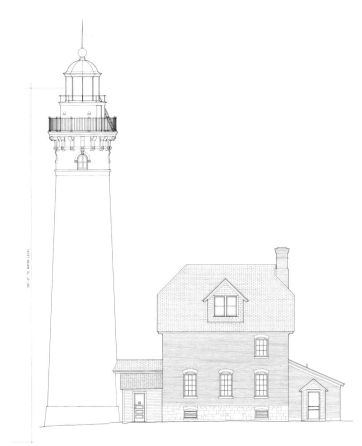

2-111

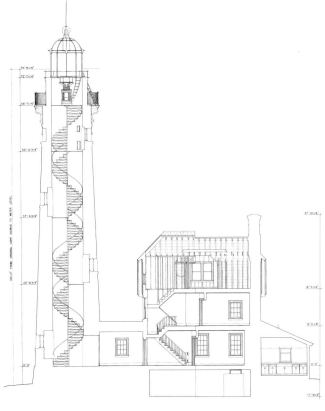

2-112

2-110. Section through Au Sable Light Station, southern shore of Lake Superior, Grand Marais Vic., Michigan. Jeff Bostetter, delineator, 1988. P&P, HABS, MICH,2-GRAMA.V,1-, sheet no. 7.

2-111. West elevation, Outer Island Lighthouse, Apostle Islands, Lapointe Vic., Wisconsin. Kenneth W. Martin, delineator, 1990. P&P, HABS, WIS,2-LPOIT.V,4A-.

2-112. Section through Outer Island Lighthouse, Lapointe Vic., Wisconsin. Daniel J. Lind, delineator, 1990. P&P, HABS, WIS,2-LPOIT.V,4A-.

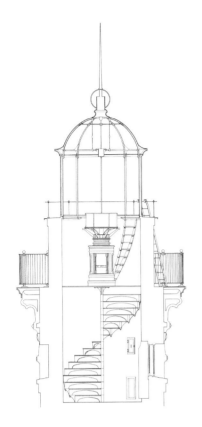

2-113

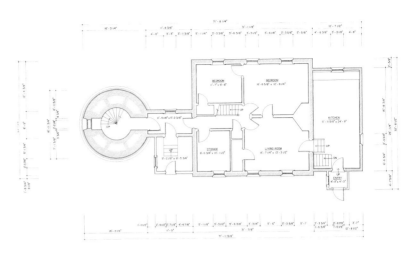

2-114

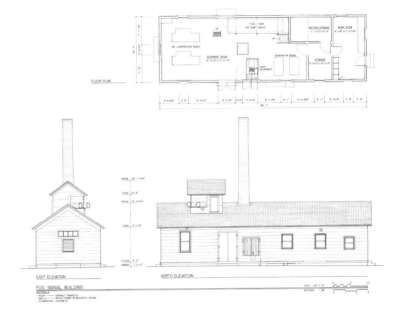

2-115

2-113. Section through the lantern, Outer Island Lighthouse, Lapointe Vic., Wisconsin. Eva H. Kunckel, delineator, 1990. P&P, HABS, WIS,2-LPOIT.V,4A-.

2-114. First floor plan, Outer Island Lighthouse, Lapointe Vic., Wisconsin. Eva H. Kunckel, delineator, 1990. P&P, HABS, WIS,2-LPOIT.V,4A-.

2-115. Fog signal building, Outer Island Lighthouse, Lapointe Vic., Wisconsin. Judith E. Collins, delineator, 1990. P&P, HABS, WIS,2-LPOIT.V,4B-.

Block Island Southeast Light in Rhode Island is another example of fine lighthouse architecture. Established in 1875, the station has a double house for two keepers and an octagonal tower. It is built of brick with stone trim. Although the tower stands only 52 feet tall, because it is situated on a high bluff it has a focal plane of 258 feet. The tower was moved back from the eroding cliff's edge in 1993.

2-116

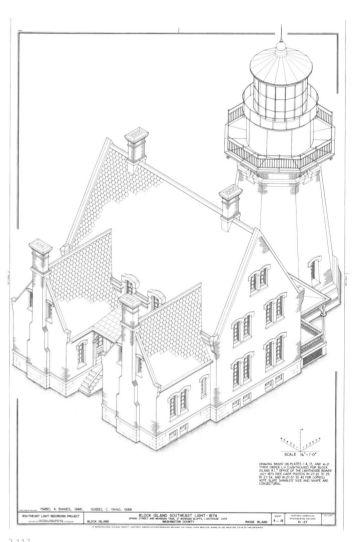

2-117

2-116. Ocean side, isometric drawing of Block Island Southeast Light Station, New Shoreham, Rhode Island. Mabel Baiges and Isabel Yang, delineators, 1988. P&P, HAER, RI,5-NESH,1-.

2-117. Land side, isometric drawing of Block Island Southeast Light Station, New Shoreham, Rhode Island. Mabel Baiges and Isabel Yang, delineators, 1988. P&P, HAER, RI,5-NESH,1-, sheet no. 5.

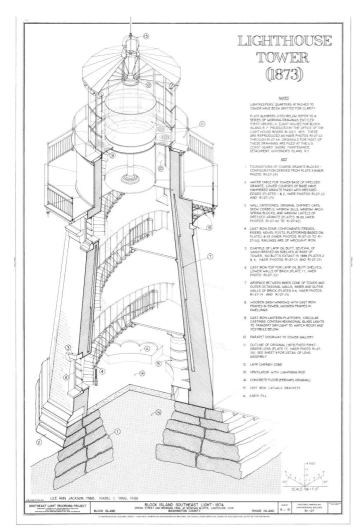

LIGHTHOUSE
TOWER
(1873)

2-118

2-119

2-120

2-118. Section through the tower, Block Island Southeast Light Station, New Shoreham, Rhode Island. Mabel Baiges and Isabel Yang, delineator, 1988. P&P, HAER, RI,5-NESH,1-.

2-119. General view of Block Island Southeast Light Station looking northwest, New Shoreham, Rhode Island. Martin Stupich, photographer, 1988. P&P, HAER, RI,5-NESH, 1-2.

2-120. General view of building front looking west, Block Island Southeast Light Station, New Shoreham, Rhode Island. Martin Stupich, photographer, 1988. P&P, HAER, RI,5-NESH, 1-1.

2-121

2-123

2-122

2-121. Side elevation, Block Island Southeast Light Station looking northwest, New Shoreham, Rhode Island. Martin Stupich, photographer, 1988. P&P, HAER, RI,5-NESH, 1-3.

2-122. Base of the iron stairway in the tower, Block Island Southeast Light Station, New Shoreham, Rhode Island. Martin Stupich, photographer, 1988. P&P, HAER, RI,5-NESH,1-14.

2-123. Inclined posts on the second floor, Block Island Southeast Light Station, New Shoreham, Rhode Island. Martin Stupich, photographer, 1988. P&P, HAER, RI,5-NESH,1-12.

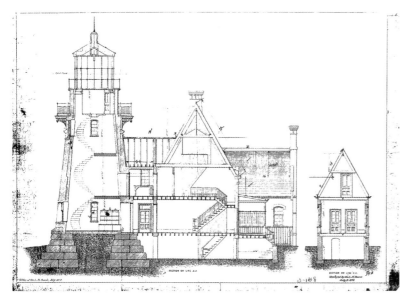

2-124

2-124. Contemporary drawing, section through the tower and dwelling, Block Island Southeast Light Station, New Shoreham, Rhode Island. 1873. Original at the U.S. Coast Guard Shore Maintenance Detachment, Governor's Island, New York, New York. P&P, HAER, RI,5-NESH,1-34.

2-125. Contemporary drawing, section of lantern with the outline of first order fixed lens, Block Island Southeast Light Station, New Shoreham, Rhode Island. 1873. Original at the U.S. Coast Guard Shore Maintenance Detachment, Governor's Island, New York, New York. P&P, HAER, RI,5-NESH,1-41.

2-126. Contemporary drawing, plan of cellar/first story, Block Island Southeast Light Station, New Shoreham, Rhode Island. 1873. Original at the U.S. Coast Guard Shore Maintenance Detachment, Governor's Island, New York, New York. P&P, HAER, RI,5-NESH, 1-36.

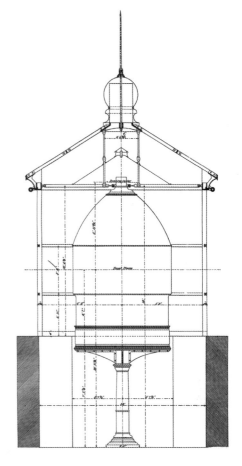

2-125

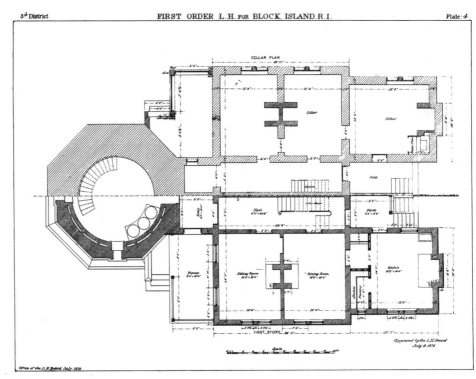

2-126

Less impressive than its contemporaries but still a handsome unit, the Thirty Mile Point Lighthouse in New York is a stone house with a square stone tower, completed in 1875. The house was extended with a brick addition at a later date.

2-127. Thirty Mile Point Lighthouse, near Barker, New York. J. Carl Burke Jr., photographer, 1970. P&P, HABS, NY,32-SOM,2-3.

2-127

Round Island Light, Michigan

Built in 1894, this brick structure consists of a three-story dwelling and a square tower. It is located on a shoal off Round Island and helped guide ships through the channel between Mackinac Island and Round Island in Lake Huron.

2-128

Square towers

Navesink Lighthouse, New Jersey

First established in 1828, the Navesink Lighthouse was a large building with towers at each end. The structure was rebuilt in 1862. Shown here is the north tower, an octagonal column with a castellated top and an unusually ornamental lantern. It is made of brown sandstone and stands 73 feet tall. The south tower is the same height and materials, but square.

2-129. Navesink Twin Lights Highlands, New Jersey. Standard Oil Co. (New Jersey), New Jersey. P&P, NYWTS, SUBJ/GEOG: LIGHT-HOUSES—NAVESINK—HIGHLANDS, NEW JERSEY.

2-129

Watch Hill Lighthouse, Rhode Island

2-130. Watch Hill Lighthouse, Watch Hill, Rhode Island. Ca. 1905. P&P, 5240.

Lighted in 1856, this square granite tower stands 45 feet tall. The site had been the location of the second lighthouse to be built in Rhode Island, a wooden tower erected 1807.

2-130

Fort Point Light, Maine

Fort Point Light, located at the mouth of the Penobscot River, is a square brick structure that was lighted in 1857 and stands 31 feet tall.

2-131. Fort Point Light Station, showing bell house, garage, keeper's house, and light tower, Stockton Springs, Maine. Richard Cheek, photographer, 1990. P&P, HABS, ME-203-2.

2-131

2-132. Fort Point Lighthouse, Stockton
Springs, Maine. Richard Cheek, photographer, 1990. P&P, HABS, ME-203-5.

2-133. Detail of lantern, Fort Point
Lighthouse, Stockton Springs, Maine.
Richard Cheek, photographer, 1990. P&P,
HABS, ME-203-7.

2-132

2-133

Burnt Coat Harbor Lighthouse, Maine

This square brick tower, 32 feet tall and built in 1872, stands at Hockamock Head on Swans Island, at the entrance to Burnt Coat Harbor. The tower was originally the rear half of range lights, but the front light was discontinued.

2-134. Burnt Coat Harbor Lighthouse and keeper's dwelling, Swans Island, Maine. Richard Cheek, photographer, 1990. P&P, HABS, ME-198-2.

2-135. Burnt Coat Harbor Lighthouse, also showing bell house (left), Swans Island, Maine. Richard Cheek, photographer, 1990. P&P, HABS, ME-198-3.

2-134

2-135

Grindle Point Lighthouse, Maine

Another square brick tower in Maine, with slightly battered walls, is found at Grindle Point. This lighthouse was built in 1874 and stands 39 feet tall.

2-136

2-136. Grindle Point Lighthouse, Maine. Richard Cheek, photographer, 1989. P&P, HABS, ME,14-ISBO,1-1.

2-137. Oil house at Grindle Point Lighthouse. Richard Cheek, photographer, 1989. P&P, HABS, ME,14-ISBO,1-12.

2-137

Hendricks Head Lighthouse, Maine

Hendricks Head Lighthouse, at the entrance to the Sheepscot River, is a square brick tower that stands 39 feet tall. Built in 1875, it is the second lighthouse on the site, replacing a cottage-style structure.

2-138. Hendricks Head Lighthouse, with the keeper's dwelling and bell house, West Southport, Maine. Richard Cheek, photographer, 1989. P&P, HABS, ME-186-2.

2-138

2-139

2-140

2-139. Hendricks Head Lighthouse, West Southport, Maine.
Richard Cheek, photographer, 1989. P&P, HABS, ME-186-4.

2-140. Stairway inside Hendricks Head Lighthouse, West
Southport, Maine. Richard Cheek, photographer, 1989. P&P,
HABS, ME-186-5.

Cylindrical towers

Narraguagus (Pond Island) Light, Maine

This lighthouse is hard to classify because what is now a cylindrical stone tower started out as part of a cottage-style structure. The tower rose from the middle of a stone house, built in 1853. Then, in 1875, the existing house was stripped away and a new, frame dwelling went up apart from the tower, which became a freestanding structure. The lighthouse stands 31 feet tall and is painted white.

2-141. Narraguagus Lighthouse and keeper's dwelling, Pond Island, Maine. Richard Cheek, photographer, 1990. P&P, HABS, ME-195-2.

2-141

Pumpkin Island Light, Maine

2-142. Pumpkin Island Lighthouse and keeper's dwelling, Sargentville, Maine. Richard Cheek, photographer, 1990. P&P, HABS, ME-200-2.

Pumpkin Island Light is a small, cylindrical brick tower, erected in 1854.

2-142

Gay Head Lighthouse, Massachusetts

Located on the island of Martha's Vineyard, Gay Head Lighthouse became operational in 1856 and replaced an earlier lighthouse. It is nearly cylindrical, made of brick and sandstone, and stands 51 feet tall. The keeper's house in picture 2-143 was demolished in 1956.

2-143. Gay Head Lighthouse, Martha's Vineyard, Massachusetts. Frank W. Small, photographer, 1953. P&P, SSF, LIGHTHOUSES–MASS.–1953, GAY HEAD LIGHT.

2-144. Gay Head Light, Martha's Vineyard, Massachusetts. Between 1900 and 1906. DPCC, LC-D4-16142.

2-143

2-144

Cape Cod (Highland) Lighthouse, Massachusetts

2-145. View from the southeast, Cape Cod (Highland) Lighthouse, Truro, Massachusetts. Cervin Robinson, photographer, 1959. P&P, HABS, MASS,1-TRU,24-1.

Another cylindrical tower located on the Massachusetts coast is this 66-foot-tall structure on the eastern side of Cape Cod near Truro. It was built in 1857. The tower was moved from its original site in 1996 to protect it from erosion.

2-145

Browns Head Light, Maine

This cylindrical brick lighthouse is only 20 feet tall. Located at the northern end of Vinalhaven Island, it went into service in 1857.

2-146. Browns Head Lighthouse and keeper's dwelling, Vinalhaven Island, Maine. Richard Cheek, photographer, 1989. P&P, HABS, ME-184-2.

2-146

Seguin Island Lighthouse, Maine

2-147. Seguin Island Lighthouse and keeper's dwelling, Seguin Island, Maine. Richard Cheek, photographer, 1991. P&P, HABS, ME-213-4.

An important lighthouse at the entrance to the Kennebec River, Seguin Island Light is a conical granite tower that went into service in 1857. It stands 53 feet tall.

2-147

Tenants Harbor Light, Maine

Standing on Southern Island at the entrance to Tenants Harbor, the lighthouse is a 27-foot-tall brick cylinder. It was lighted on January 1, 1858.

2-148. Tenants Harbor Lighthouse and keeper's dwelling, Southern Island, Maine. Richard Cheek, photographer, 1989. P&P, HABS, ME-215-3.

2-148

Bass Harbor Head Light, Maine

Another small, cylindrical brick lighthouse, Bass Harbor Head Light stands 32 feet tall and went into service in 1858. It is located at the southern end of Mt. Desert Island, marking the entrance to Bass Harbor and the Blue Hill Bay.

2-149

Great Duck Island Lighthouse, Maine

The lighthouse at Great Duck Island, out in the Atlantic Ocean about 6 miles from Mount Desert Island, marks the entrance to Blue Hill Bay and the Mount Desert Island area. The lighthouse, which became operational in 1890, is a brick cylinder that stands 42 feet tall.

2-150. Great Duck Island Lighthouse, Great Duck Island, Maine. Richard Cheek, photographer, 1991. P&P, HABS, ME-207-4.

2-150

Curtis Island Light, Maine

Lighted in 1896, this small, cylindrical brick structure replaced an earlier lighthouse. It stood 25 feet tall. Originally named Negro Island, the island was renamed in 1934 in honor of Cyrus H. K. Curtis, publisher of the *Saturday Evening Post* and a summer resident of Camden, Maine.

2-151

2-152

2-151. Curtis Island Lighthouse and keeper's dwelling, Curtis Island, near Camden, Maine. Richard Cheek, photographer, 1991. P&P, HABS, ME-220-3.

2-152. Curtis Island Lighthouse, Curtis Island, near Camden, Maine. Richard Cheek, photographer, 1991. P&P, HABS, ME-220-5.

Annisquam Light, Massachusetts

In 1897 this cylindrical brick tower went into service. It stands 41 feet tall and is painted white.

2-153. Annisquam Light, Gloucester, Massachusetts. Between 1900 and 1920. DPCC, LC-D4-60X.

2-153

Cleveland Harbor Lighthouses, Ohio

2-154. Entrance to Cleveland Harbor, Ohio. Ca. 1905. DPCC, LC-D4-18624.

2-155. Lighthouse and life-saving station on a pier in Cleveland Harbor, Ohio. Between 1910 and 1920. DPCC, LC-D4-72384.

This pair of cylindrical lighthouses stood on the ends of piers.

2-154

2-155

2-156

2-156. Life-saving station and lighthouse on a pier in Cleveland Harbor, Ohio. Ca. 1905. DPCC, LC-D4-18625.

Ornamental forms

Welfare Island Lighthouse, New York

This lighthouse on Welfare (now Roosevelt) Island was built by the City of New York in 1872. The 50-foot-tall stone tower was designed by James Renwick Jr., a prominent New York architect.

2-157. Welfare Island Lighthouse, New York City, New York. Jack Boucher, photographer, 1970. P&P, HABS, NY,31-WELFI,3-1.

2-157

Bois Blanc Park Lighthouse, Michigan

The lighthouse appears to be growing in a field.

2-158. Lighthouse, Bois Blanc Park, Michigan. Between 1900 and 1906. DPCC, LC-D4-16727.

2-158

San Francisco Lighthouse, California

2-159. San Francisco City Lighthouse, California. International News Photo, 1933. P&P, NYWTS, SUBJ/GEOG: LIGHTOUSES—SAN FRANCISCO—CALIFORNIA.

A few private aids to navigation have existed alongside the national lighthouses. For example, the City of San Francisco built this lighthouse to mark the entrance to a yacht harbor. It is made of old rocks and cobblestones that were taken up from the city's streets when they were repaved.

2-159

COTTAGE-STYLE

DWELLING WITH INTEGRAL TOWER

LIGHTHOUSES

An early form of lighthouse, cottage-style lighthouses consist of a tower and lantern integrated with a dwelling. They were made of masonry, wood, and iron, although sometimes the tower and dwelling were built of different materials (example, a masonry house with a wood tower). The tower's location could vary: it might be at one end of the building, or in the center, or projecting somewhat from it, like the steeple of a church. It is unknown how many of this type were ever built, but few survive. They were built on the East Coast, in California, and on shores between the coasts.

Selkirk (Salmon River) Lighthouse, New York

Established in 1838 at the junction of the Salmon River at Lake Ontario, the Selkirk (Salmon River) Lighthouse is a two-story stone house with an attic and a wooden tower in the gable end of the roof. It has one of few old-style lanterns still in existence.

3-001. Selkirk (Salmon River) Lighthouse, New Pulaski, New York. P&P, HABS, NY,38-PORTO.V,1-2.

3-002. Selkirk (Salmon River) Lighthouse, New Pulaski, New York. P&P, HABS, NY,38-PORTO.V,1-1.

3-001

3-002

Old Point Loma Lighthouse, California

Old Point Loma Lighthouse, completed in 1855, was among the first group of U.S. government–built lighthouses in California, and the last of this group to be completed. The sandstone house measured 20 feet wide and 38 feet long and had a cistern in the cellar. The tower, in the center of the building, was brick. Although the light itself was only 38 feet off the ground, its situation on a high bluff gave it a focal plane of 433 feet. Decommissioned in 1891, the lighthouse is now part of the Cabrillo National Monument.

3-003. East side (front), Old Point Loma Lighthouse, San Diego, California. Early 1880s. P&P, HABS, CAL,37-POLO,1-1.

3-004. West side, Old Point Loma Lighthouse, San Diego, California. Taken before March 1891. P&P, HABS, CAL,37-POLO,1-2.

3-005. Ship ladder and hatchway leading from the tower room to the lantern, Old Point Loma Lighthouse, San Diego, California. H. C. White, photographer, 1934. P&P, HABS, CAL,37-POLO,1-16.

3-005

3-003

3-004

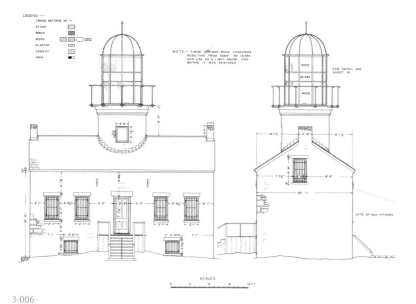

3-006

3-007

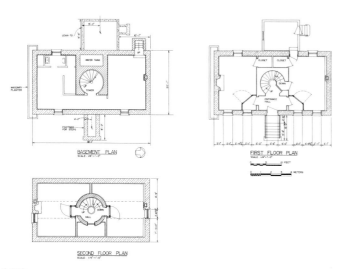

3-008

3-006. East (front) and north elevation, Old Point Loma Lighthouse, San Diego, California. James G. Langdon, delineator, 1934. P&P, HABS, CAL,37-POLO,1-.

3-007. Section through center looking north (left) and looking west (right), Old Point Loma Lighthouse, San Diego, California. James G. Langdon, delineator, 1934. P&P, HABS, CAL,37-POLO,1-.

3-008. Basement, first, and second floor plans, Old Point Loma Lighthouse, San Diego, California. B. Santos, delineator, 1935. P&P, HABS, CAL,37-POLO,1-, sheet no. 2.

Harbor Point Lighthouse, Michigan

3-009. Harbor Point Lighthouse, Harbor Springs, Michigan. Ca. 1900. DPCC, LC-D4-12310.

This cottage-style lighthouse, date of construction unknown, was located on Lake Michigan at Little Traverse Bay.

3-009

Jones Point Lighthouse, Virginia

Lighted in 1856, the Jones Point Lighthouse on the Potomac River in Virginia is a rare surviving example of a wood-frame house with a tower. The building measures about 19 by 39 feet, with the lantern located in the center, over a hall with a stairway to it. When the structure was photographed in 1963 it was in derelict condition, but it since has been restored.

3-010. Jones Point Lighthouse, Jones Point, Potomac River, Virginia. 1963. P&P, HABS, VA,7-ALEX.V,2-1.

3-010

3-011. First floor plan, Jones Point
Lighthouse, Jones Point, Potomac River,
Virginia. Kenneth Clark, delineator, 1963.
P&P, HABS, VA,7-ALEX.V,2, sheet no. 3.

3-012. South elevation reconstruction
study, Jones Point Lighthouse, Jones Point,
Potomac River, Virginia. John A. Matthews,
delineator, 1963. P&P, HABS, VA,7-
ALEX.V,2, sheet no. 5.

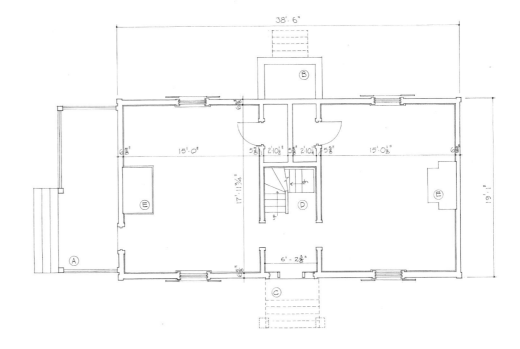

FIRST FLOOR PLAN
SCALE: 1/4"=1'-0"

3-011

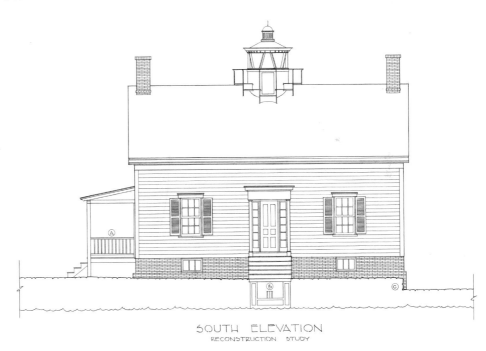

SOUTH ELEVATION
RECONSTRUCTION STUDY

3-012

Michigan City Lighthouse, Indiana

Indiana's only aid to navigation, the old Michigan City Lighthouse on Lake Michigan was lighted in 1858. It was adapted to serve as a keeper's dwelling in 1904 when a new lighthouse replaced it. At that time, an addition to the north side of the building doubled its size, to about 31 by 49 feet; the whole structure was remodeled and porches were added. Thus, the drawings, which predate the building's restoration, do not show the tower and lantern, which were replicated and placed on the building in 1973. It is two and half stories with brick walls that are covered with wood shingles at the second story.

3-013. East elevation showing the Michigan City Lighthouse after remodeling in 1904, Michigan City, Indiana. Patrick Kelley, delineator. P&P, HABS, IND,46-MICI,1-, sheet no. 6.

3-014. Second floor plan with the 1904 addition, Michigan City Lighthouse, Michigan City, Indiana. Patrick Kelley, delineator. P&P, HABS, IND,46-MICI,1-, sheet no. 4.

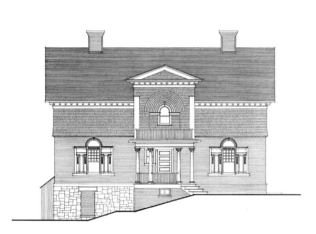

3-013

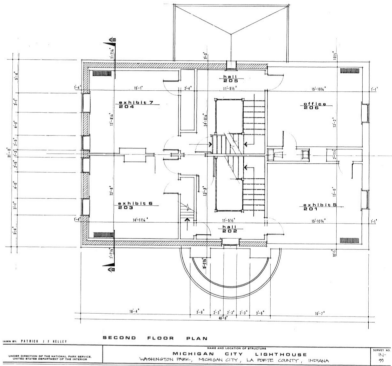

3-014

Raspberry Island Light, Wisconsin

3-015. West elevation, Raspberry Island Lighthouse, Bayfield Vic., Wisconsin. Lisa Monnig, delineator, 1989. P&P, HABS, WIS,4-BAYF.V,2A-, sheet no. 4.

3-016. South elevation and section. Raspberry Island Lighthouse, Bayfield Vic., Wisconsin. Richard Naab, delineator, 1989. P&P, HABS, WIS,4-BAYF.V,2A-, sheet no. 6.

Located on one of the Apostle Islands in Lake Superior, the Raspberry Island Lighthouse was built in 1863, and remodeled and enlarged in 1906. The building is a wood-frame structure with an attached, 35-foot-tall tower.

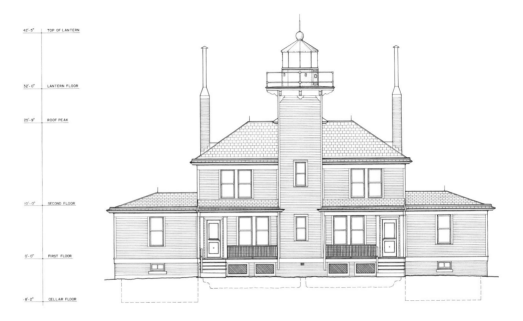

3-015

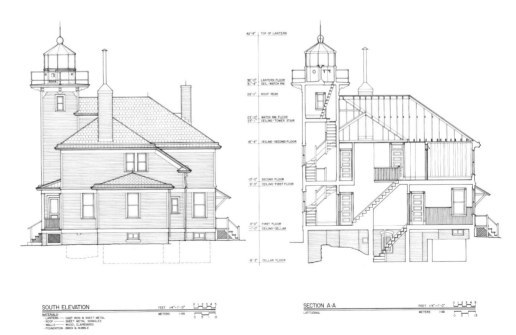

3-016

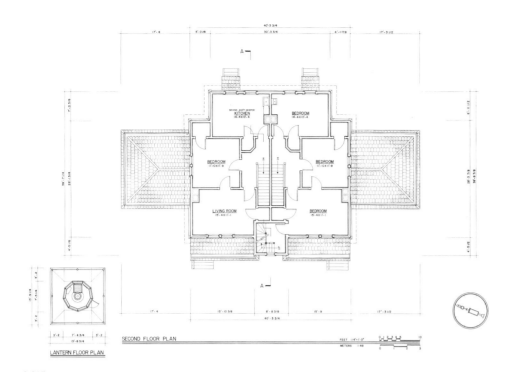

3-017

3-017. Second floor plan, Raspberry Island Lighthouse, Bayfield Vic., Wisconsin. Gary R. Stephens, delineator, 1989. P&P, HABS, WIS,4-BAYF.V,2A-, sheet no. 3.

3-018. Fog signal building, Raspberry Island Lighthouse, Bayfield Vic., Wisconsin. Douglas R. Wighell, delineator, 1989. P&P, HABS, WIS,4-BAYF.V,2B-.

3-018

Copper Harbor (Old) Lighthouse, Michigan

Copper Harbor (Old) Lighthouse, a brick cottage with a 42-foot-tall square tower projecting from an end wall, was erected in 1866 on the site of one of the first lighthouses on Lake Superior. The structure, was deactivated in 1933 when a new skeleton tower went into operation (see 7-015 and 7-016).

3-019

Block Island North Lighthouse, Rhode Island

This granite lighthouse with an octagonal iron tower on one end went into operation in 1867. It is the fourth lighthouse on the site.

3-020. "Old" lighthouse on Block Island, Rhode Island. 1876. Gen. Coll., *Harper's New Monthly Magazine* 53, no. 314 (July 1876): 170.

3-020

Old Field Point Lighthouse, New York

3-021. Old Field Point Lighthouse, Old Field, Long Island, New York. B. J. E. Rowell, photographer. P&P, SSF, LIGHTHOUSES—NEW YORK.

Built in 1868, the Old Field Point Light was a two-story stone house with a wooden tower. It was physically similar to the Block Island North Light, completed the year before.

3-021

Rose Island Lighthouse, Rhode Island

Established in 1870, this wooden lighthouse stands on the circular bastion of an eighteenth-century fort on Rose Island, near Newport, Rhode Island. Like many cottage-style lighthouses, the tower has chamfered corners, which create an octagonal shape.

3-022. Rose Island Lighthouse, near Newport, Rhode Island. Jet Lowe, photographer, 2000. P&P, HAER, RI-57-1.

3-022

Colchester Reef Light, Vermont

Once located on Lake Champlain, the Colchester Reef Light was architecturally similar to the contemporaneous Rose Island Lighthouse (3-022), including the octagonal tower. The Colchester Reef Light was completed in 1871, deactivated in 1933, and moved to the Shelburne Museum.

3-023

Ship Canal Lighthouse, Michigan

This was one of identical twin lighthouses erected at the end of the then-new Ship Canal at Lake St. Clair; the structure was lighted 1871. The octagonal tower and keeper's house was brick. It was accessible only by boat.

3-024. Lighthouse at end of ship canal, St. Clair Lake, Michigan. Frances Benjamin Johnston, photographer, 1903. FBJC, LC-USZ61-1386.

3-024

Hereford Inlet Lighthouse, New Jersey

3-025. West and south elevations, Hereford Inlet Lighthouse, North Wildwood, New Jersey. James Garrison, delineator, 1981. P&P, HABS, NJ1238.

3-026. North elevation and section, Hereford Inlet Lighthouse, North Wildwood, New Jersey. James Garrison, delineator, 1981. P&P, HABS, NJ1238.

Hereford Inlet Lighthouse (1874) is a square wooden tower in the center of a two-story wooden house.

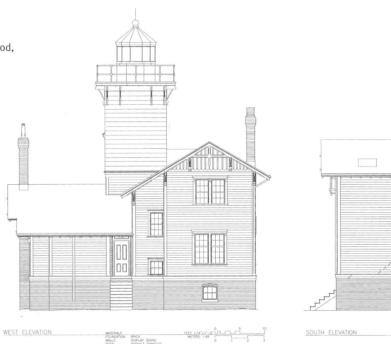

WEST ELEVATION

SOUTH ELEVATION

3-025

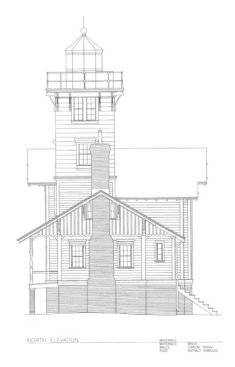

NORTH ELEVATION

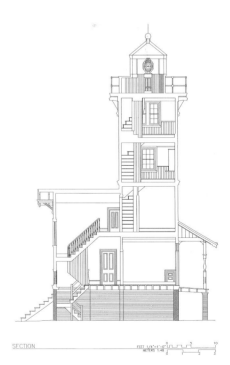

SECTION

3-026

Egg Rock Lighthouse, Maine

Located in the entrance to Frenchman Bay, Egg Rock is a tiny Maine islet with a lighthouse. The lighthouse, which became operational in 1875, is a square brick tower in the center of a wood-frame house one and a half stories tall. The roof of the house was modified in 1899, when dormer windows were added.

3-027. Egg Rock Lighthouse and fog signal building, Egg Rock (near Bar Harbor), Maine. Richard Cheek, photographer, 1992. P&P, HABS, ME,5-WIHA.V,2-1.

3-028. Egg Rock Lighthouse, Egg Rock (near Bar Harbor), Maine. Richard Cheek, photographer, 1992. P&P, HABS, ME,5-WIHA.V.2-4.

3-027

3-028

Sand Island Lighthouse, Wisconsin

3-029. Elevation, Sand Island Lighthouse, Bayfield Vic., Wisconsin. Douglas R. Mighell, delineator, 1989. P&P, HABS, WIS,4-BAYF.V,3A-, sheet no. 3.

3-030. Section through tower and house, Sand Island Lighthouse, Bayfield Vic., Wisconsin. Gary R. Stephens, delineator, 1989. P&P, HABS, WIS,4-BAYF.V,3A-, sheet no. 4.

3-031. Plan of Sand Island Lighthouse, Bayfield Vic., Wisconsin. Lisa Monnig, delineator, 1989. P&P, HABS, WIS,4-BAYF.V,3A-, sheet no. 1.

The Sand Island Lighthouse (lighted in 1881) is architecturally similar to the Ship Canal Lighthouse (3-024), except it is built of brown sandstone. The following year another lighthouse of a very similar design, the Passage Island Lighthouse (3-032–3-034), was built off Isle Royale in Michigan.

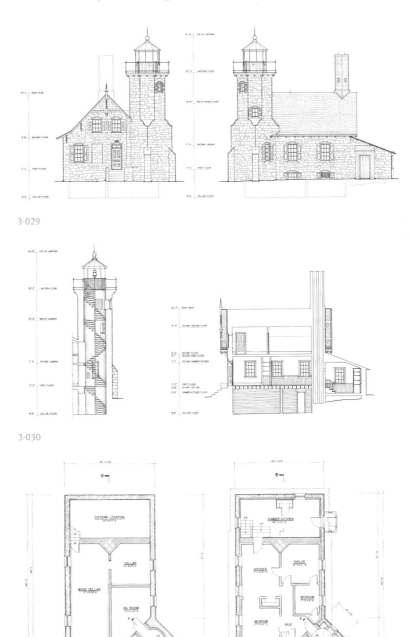

3-029

3-030

3-031

Passage Island Lighthouse, Michigan

Completed in 1882, the year after Sand Island Lighthouse, Passage Island Light looks like its Great Lakes neighbor except that it is built of fieldstone. Located off Isle Royale, the tower is 44 feet tall.

3-032. Southwest and southeast elevations, Passage Island Lighthouse, Passage Island off Isle Royale, Michigan. Denise A. Hopkins and David E. Naill, delineators, 1992. P&P, HABS, MICH,42-COPHAR.V,1A.

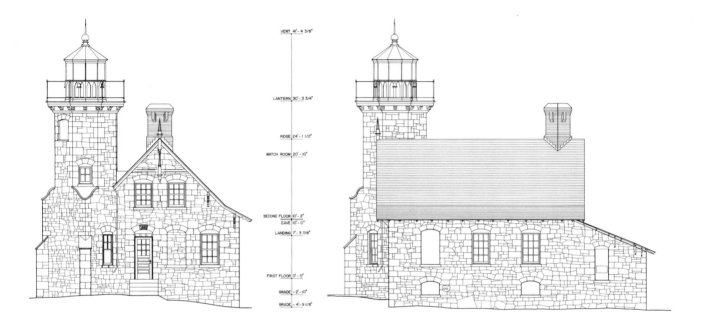

3-032

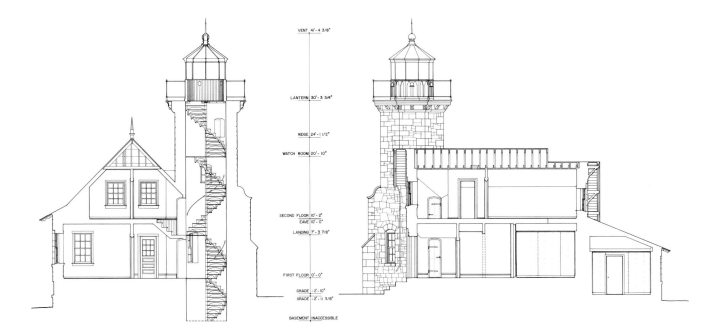

3-033

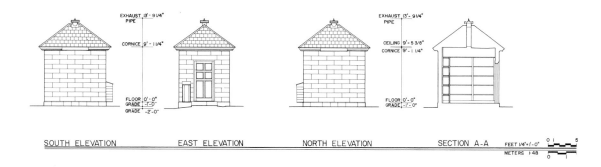

SOUTH ELEVATION   EAST ELEVATION   NORTH ELEVATION   SECTION A-A   FEET 1/4"=1'-0"
    METERS 1:48

3-034

3-033. Sections through Passage Island
Lighthouse, Passage Island off Isle Royale,
Michigan. David E. Naill, delineator, 1992.
P&P, HABS, MICH,42-COPHAR.V,1A-.

3-034. Oil storage building at Passage
Island Light Station, Passage Island off Isle
Royale, Michigan. Denise A. Hopkins, delin-
eator, 1992. P&P, HABS, MICH,42-
COPHAR.V,1C-.

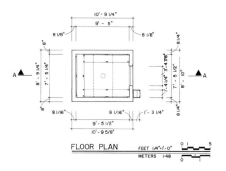

FLOOR PLAN   FEET 1/4"=1'-0"
    METERS 1:48

Cedar Point Lighthouse, Maryland

Standing on an island near where the Patuxent River enters the Chesapeake Bay, the Cedar Point Lighthouse was completed in 1896. The brick and wood-frame building measured about 27 by 33 feet. However, the site became inundated with water, and the abandoned building was well on its way to collapse when it was photographed in 1981. The lantern and its base were salvaged in 1981 and brought to the Naval Air Station's Naval Air Test and Evaluation Museum, Patuxent River, Maryland. In 1996 the upper part of the building—the wooden third floor and roof—was lifted by a huge crane, placed on a barge, and delivered to the Calvert Marine Museum. A radar reflector now occupies the lighthouse's former site.

3-035. South view, Cedar Point Lighthouse, Cedar Point at the Patuxent River and the Chesapeake Bay, Maryland. Chesapeake Division, Naval Facilities Engineering Command, photographer, 1981. P&P, HABS, MD,19-LEXP.V,1-1.

3-035

3-036. Second floor (interior), Cedar Point Lighthouse, Cedar Point at the Patuxent River and the Chesapeake Bay, Maryland. Chesapeake Division, Naval Facilities Engineering Command, photographer, 1981. P&P, HABS, MD,19-LEXP.V,1-12.

3-037. Detail of ceiling in tower, Cedar Point Lighthouse, Cedar Point at the Patuxent River and the Chesapeake Bay, Maryland. Chesapeake Division, Naval Facilities Engineering Command, photographer, 1981. P&P, HABS, MD,19-LEXP.V,1-18.

3-036

3-037

CAST-IRON PLATE LIGHTHOUSES

Early lighthouse architects used iron in various minor ways—for example, in the lantern frames. At the opening of the nineteenth century, iron was too costly a material to use on a large scale. In the 1840s the nation's output of iron increased greatly, and for the first time designers used iron for entire structures. The cast-iron plate lighthouse was the first type of all-iron lighthouse in the United States. Made of sections of cast iron bolted together and generally lined with brick, these towers had many advantages: they were durable, noncombustible, and weighed less than masonry buildings of similar dimensions — a desirable feature for sites with compressible ground or for a pier. Cast-iron could be readily molded, and iron towers took various forms, including conical, cylindrical, and octagonal. They were prefabricated, which meant they could be disassembled, moved, and rebuilt at a new site. This feature made them well suited for locations where materials were difficult to obtain, which is why the British, who invented the form, used them for sites in their colonies.

Long Island Head Lighthouse, erected in 1844 in Boston Harbor in Massachusetts, was the first cast-iron plate tower in the United States. The structure (no longer extant) was cast and fabricated by Cyrus Alger & Co.'s South Boston Iron Company in Boston, Massachusetts, and it stood 34 feet tall. Most of the cast-iron plate lighthouses that are still standing were built in the 1870s and 1880s.

Gibbs Hill, Bermuda, and Morant Point, Jamaica, Lighthouses

British engineers built cast-iron lighthouses at Gibbs Hill, Bermuda, and Morant Point, Jamaica. The Gibbs Hill tower stood 133 feet 9 inches from the base to the top of the lantern. Its lenticular apparatus, at £5,500, cost 25 percent more than the entire tower itself. The Morant Point tower stood 101 feet 6 inches. Both had small bases relative to their height: the former had a 24-foot-diameter base that tapered to a 12-foot 6-inch gallery, and the latter had an 18-foot 6-inch diameter base tapering to an 11-foot gallery.

4-001. Gibbs Hill, Bermuda, and Morant Point, Jamaica, lighthouses. 1846. Gen. Coll., plate 25, volume of plates accompanying the *Report . . . on improvements in the light-house system . . .*, Senate doc. No. 488 29:1.

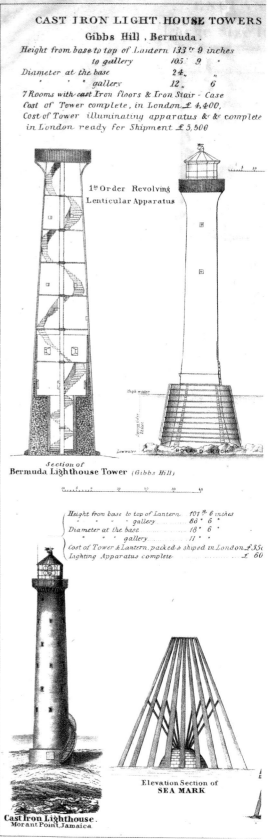

4-001

Biloxi Lighthouse, Mississippi

An extant, early cast-iron plate tower, the Biloxi Lighthouse on the Mississippi Sound was completed in 1848. It stands 61 feet tall and is notable for retaining an old-style lantern.

4-002. Biloxi Lighthouse, Biloxi, Mississippi. Ca. 1901. DPCC, P&P, LC-D4-13538.

4-003. Biloxi Lighthouse, Biloxi, Mississippi. WC, P&P, SSF, LIGHTHOUSES—MISSISSIPPI, BILOXI LIGHTHOUSE, BILOXI, MISS.

4-002

4-003

Monomoy Point Light, Massachusetts

Like the first American cast-iron lighthouse, this one was built by Cyrus Alger & Co. of Boston and was lighted in 1849. It was designed as a cylindrical structure and looks rather top-heavy because it has a large lantern on a narrow tower. Indeed, the lighthouse had to be braced by various means over the years: heavy wooden braces and guy wires or chains, as well as a metal framework at a later date. Now the 40-foot-tall structure stands without them. It replaced an earlier cottage-style tower.

4-004. View of Monomoy Point Lighthouse, Chatham, Massachusetts. Gerald Weinstein, photographer, 1987. P&P, HAER, MASS,1-CHAT,6-2.

opposite
4-005. Monomoy Point Lighthouse, Chatham, Massachusetts. Gerald Weinstein, photographer, 1987. P&P, HAER, MASS,1-CHAT,6-5.

4-004

4-005

4-006

4-007

4-008

4-006. Base of the lighthouse at Monomoy, Chatham, Massachusetts. Gerald Weinstein, photographer, 1987. P&P, HAER, MASS,1-CHAT,6-6.

4-007. Detail showing the plates of the tower, Monomoy Point Lighthouse, Chatham, Massachusetts. Gerald Weinstein, photographer, 1987. P&P, HAER, MASS,1-CHAT,6-7.

4-008. Interior of tower showing the brick lining and stairs, Monomoy Point Lighthouse, Chatham, Massachusetts. Gerald Weinstein, photographer, 1987. P&P, HAER, MASS,1-CHAT,6-8.

Point Reyes Light, Point Reyes, California

Designs for the first lighthouses in California, authorized in the 1850s, were cottage-style, but because of delays in constructing the lighthouse at Point Reyes, that structure took a different form. By the time it was built in 1870, it was a cast-iron plate tower. This squat, conical tower rises only 18 1/2 feet to the lantern gallery. However, since it stands on a high promontory, its beam is 294 feet above sea level.

4-009. Point Reyes Lighthouse soon after it was completed, looking west, Point Reyes, California. Eadweard Muybridge, photographer, ca. 1871. P&P, S, lot 13506.

4-010. Point Reyes Lighthouse, Point Reyes, California. Richard Frear, photographer, 1982. P&P, HABS, CAL,21-POREY,1-2.

4-009

4-010

4-011

4-012

4-011. Point Reyes Lighthouse, Point Reyes, California. Richard Frear, photographer, 1982. P&P, HABS, CAL,21-POREY,1-4.

4-012. Interior at ground level showing the post that supports the lens and the stairway, Point Reyes Lighthouse, Point Reyes, California. Richard Frear, photographer, 1982. P&P, HABS, CAL,21-POREY,1-5.

4-013. Sections through the Point Reyes Lighthouse, Point Reyes, California. B. Santos and N. Camarena, delineators. P&P, HABS, CAL,21-POREY,1-, sheet no. 1.

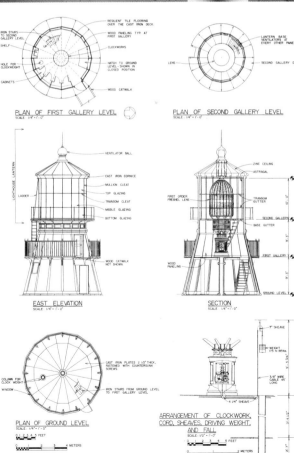

4-013

Point Bolivar Lighthouse, Texas

Built in 1872, the Point Bolivar Lighthouse consists of a cast-iron shell around a brick cylinder. It is 116 feet tall.

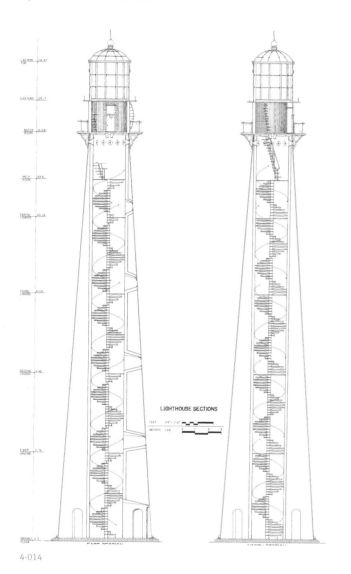

4-014

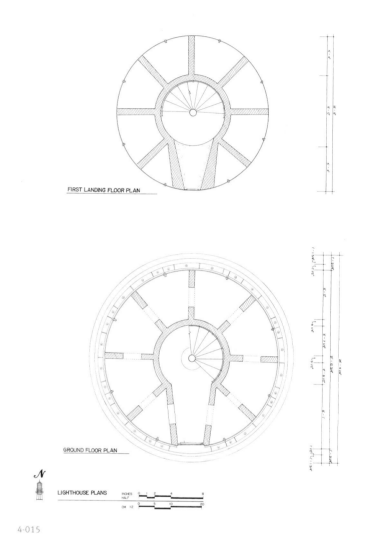

4-015

4-014. Sections through Point Bolivar Lighthouse, Galveston, Texas. Kathryn A. St. Clair, delineator, 2001. P&P, HABS, unprocessed, survey number HABS TX-3517, sheet no. 7.

4-015. Ground and first floor plans, Point Bolivar Lighthouse, Galveston, Texas. Kathryn A. St. Clair, delineator, 2001. P&P, HABS, unprocessed, survey number HABS TX-3517, sheet no. 3.

Cape Elizabeth Lighthouse, Maine

The cast-iron twin lights at Cape Elizabeth, marking the southern entrance to Casco Bay and Portland Harbor, were built in 1874 to replace two earlier towers. They were both 67 feet tall and stood 300 yards apart. In 1924 the west tower was taken out of service.

4-016

4-017

4-016. Cape Elizabeth (Twin) Lights, with inactive west tower in the foreground, near Cape Elizabeth, Maine. Richard Cheek, photographer, 1989. P&P, HABS, ME-182-1.

4-017. Cape Elizabeth (Twin) Lights, active east tower and keeper's dwelling, near Cape Elizabeth, Maine. Richard Cheek, photographer, 1989. P&P, HABS, ME-182-4.

Portland Breakwater (Bug) Lighthouse, Maine

Modeled on a classical monument, the Choragic Monument of Lysicrates in Athens, this lighthouse went into service in 1875, during the period that architect Paul Pelz (see 2-105–2-127) served as chief draftsman for the Light-House Board. The structure was deactivated in 1942.

4-018. West side, Portland Breakwater Lighthouse, South Portland, Maine. Gerda Peterich, photographer, 1962. P&P, HABS, ME,3-PORTS,1-2.

4-018

Edgartown Harbor Lighthouse, Massachusetts

4-019. Edgartown Harbor Lighthouse, Edgartown Harbor at eastern end of Martha's Vineyard, Massachusetts. Frank W. Small, photographer, 1953. P&P, SSF, LIGHTHOUSES—MASS.—1953, EDGARTOWN LIGHT.

Although placed at the Edgartown site in 1939, the Edgartown Harbor Lighthouse is actually an 1875 tower that was moved from Ipswich, Massachusetts, to replace a lighthouse destroyed in a 1938 hurricane. In Ipswich it served as part of a pair of range lights. The conical cast-iron tower stands 45 feet tall.

4-019

Hunting Island Light, South Carolina

The second lighthouse on Hunting Island, which guided ships seeking the harbor at Beaufort, was completed in 1875. This tall tower rises about 121 feet to the center of the lantern and measures about 27 feet in diameter at the base, narrowing to about 13 feet at the level below the gallery. It was made of many small cast-iron plates and had cast-iron window frames, door frames, brackets for the gallery, and interior stairs. The date the building was authorized, 1873, is over the doorway.

This tower had an opportunity to demonstrate one of the advertised advantages of cast-iron plate lighthouses: the ability to be disassembled and moved. Not long after the tower was completed, water began to wash uncomfortably close to the light station. Finally, in 1889, the lighthouse was disassembled and moved about a mile and a half south of the original site. It was re-lighted that same year.

4-020. General view of Hunting Island Lighthouse looking east, Hunting Island, South Carolina. Jack Boucher, photographer, 1986–1987. P&P, HABS, SC,7-HUNTIL,1A-1.

4-021. Top of Hunting Island Lighthouse, Hunting Island, South Carolina. Jack Boucher, photographer, 1986–1987. P&P, HABS, SC,7-HUNTIL,1A-9.

4-020

4-021

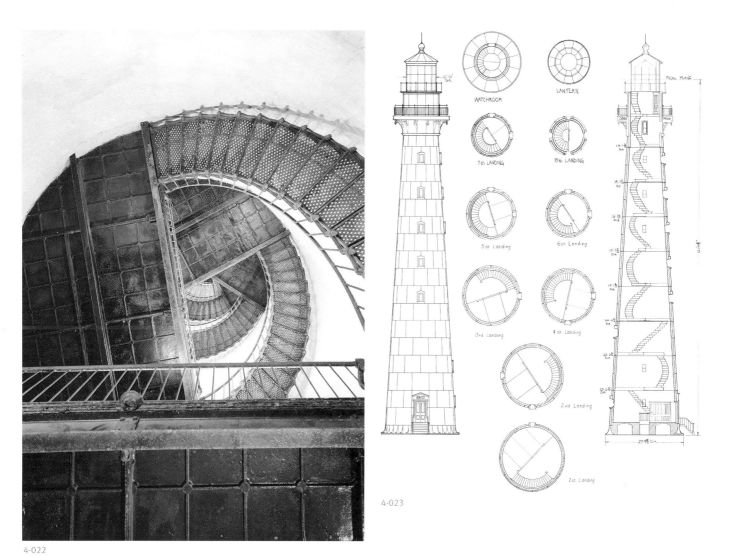

4-022

4-022. View of stairway showing weight loop on platform, Hunting Island Lighthouse, Hunting Island, South Carolina. Jack Boucher, photographer, 1986–1987. P&P, HABS, SC,7-HUNTIL,1A-15.

4-023. Elevation and section, Hunting Island Lighthouse, Hunting Island, South Carolina. J. F. Watson and R. D. Alderman, delineators, ca. 1983. P&P, HABS, SC,7-HUNTIL,1A-, sheet no. 1.

Little River Lighthouse, Maine

The first lighthouse at the Little River, built on Little River Island at the entrance to Cutler Harbor, was a cottage-style structure consisting of a rectangular stone house with a tower embedded in an end wall. In 1876 the building was converted to a dwelling exclusively and the top of the tower was removed. A new, cast-iron tower was erected; it was nearly cylindrical and stood 41 feet tall. A frame building later replaced the old dwelling.

4-024. Little River Lighthouse and keeper's dwelling, Little River Island (near Cutler), Maine. Richard Cheek, photographer, 1991. P&P, HABS, ME-216-2.

4-024

4-025

4-026

4-025. Little River Lighthouse, Little River Island (near Cutler), Maine. Richard Cheek, photographer, 1991. P&P, HABS, ME-216-4.

4-026. Interior of second floor, Little River Lighthouse, Little River Island (near Cutler), Maine. Richard Cheek, photographer, 1991. P&P, HABS, ME-216-6.

Portsmouth Harbor (New Castle) Lighthouse, New Hampshire

The 48-foot-tall tower at Portsmouth Harbor, erected on the foundation of the previous tower, was lighted in 1877.

4-027. Portsmouth Harbor Lighthouse, New Castle, New Hampshire. Between 1900 and 1910. DPCC, LC-D4-71528.

4-027

Chatham Lighthouse, Massachusetts

Originally one of twin lighthouses on the southern coast of Cape Cod that marked the entry to Chatham Harbor, the Chatham Lighthouse (1877) stands 48 feet tall.

4-028

4-029

4-028. Chatham Lighthouse, Chatham, Massachusetts. American Airlines, 1948. P&P, NYWTS, SUBJ/GEOG: LIGHTHOUSES–CAPE COD–CAPE COD, MASS-ACHUSETTS.

4-029. Chatham Lighthouse, Chatham, Massachusetts. WC, P&P, SSF, LIGHTHOUSES—MASS.—CHATHAM, MASS.

Cape Neddick ("The Nubble") Light, Maine

Located on an island off Cape Neddick called The Nubble, this lighthouse, like Little River Light of a few years earlier (4-024–4-026), is a cast-iron plate, nearly cylindrical tower standing 41 feet tall. It was lighted in 1879.

4-030. Cape Neddick Light Station, York Beach, Maine. Ca. 1904. DPCC, LC-D4-33270.

4-030

4-031. Cape Neddick Light Station, York Beach, Maine. Ca. 1900. DPCC, LC-D4-13963.

4-032. Similar view of The Nubble as above, artistically interpreted, near York Beach, Maine. 1882. Gen. Coll., *Harper's New Monthly Magazine* 65 (Sept. 1882).

4-033. The Nubble with the Cape Neddick Lighthouse, York Beach, Maine. Ca. 1901. DPCC, LC-D4-13961.

4-031

4-032

4-033

4-034

4-034. Boat house, keeper's dwelling, and light tower at Cape Neddick Light Station, York Beach, Maine. Richard Cheek, photographer, 1989. P&P, HABS, ME-192-1.

4-035. Shed and light tower, Cape Neddick Light Station, York Beach, Maine. Richard Cheek, photographer, 1989. P&P, HABS, ME-192-6.

4-035

Jeffrey's Hook Lighthouse, New York

Erected in 1880, Jeffrey's Hook Light originally stood at Sandy Hook in New Jersey. In 1921 it was moved to its current site on the Hudson River in New York City. Later the George Washington Bridge was built around it. The lighthouse was the subject of a popular children's book, *The Little Red Lighthouse and the Great Gray Bridge* by Hildegarde H. Swift (1942), and when the Coast Guard sought to remove it in 1951 an outcry from children led to its preservation.

4-036

4-037

4-036. Jeffrey's Hook Lighthouse, New York, New York. 1962. P&P, NYWTS, SUBJ/GEOG: LIGHTHOUSES–JEFFREY'S HOOK–NEW YORK CITY–HUDSON RIVER.

4-037. Jeffrey's Hook Light (little red lighthouse), New York, New York. Lynd Ward, illustrator, 1942. Gen. Coll., Hildegarde H. Swift and Lynd Ward, *The Little Red Lighthouse and the Great Gray Bridge* (New York: Harcourt Brace & Co., 1942).

New Cape Henry Lighthouse, Virginia

New Cape Henry Lighthouse is an example of a very tall cast-iron tower. At 163 feet tall, it is the tallest cast-iron plate tower, as well as one of the country's tallest towers. Fabrication of this first order light started in 1879, and it became operational in 1881. Like its masonry predecessor, which still stands, the new lighthouse had an octagonal shape. It was formed of two shells—an outer one of cast iron and an inner, wrought-iron cylinder—and was bolted to a concrete platform. It is painted with black and white vertical stripes.

4-038. Cape Henry lighthouses, new tower (left) 1881 and old tower (right) 1792, Virginia Beach, Virginia. Ca. 1905. DPCC, LC-D4-18399.

4-039. Cape Henry Lighthouse, Virginia Beach, Virginia. ACME, Photo, 1936. P&P, NYWTS, SUBJ/GEOG: LIGHTHOUSES— CAPE HENRY—VIRGINIA.

4-039

4-038

Devils Island Lighthouse, Wisconsin

4-040. Elevation, Devils Island Lighthouse, Lapointe Vic., Wisconsin. Leonard H. Simpson IV, delineator, 1991. P&P, HABS, WIS,2-LPOIT.V,1A-.

4-041. Ground plan, Devils Island Lighthouse, Lapointe Vic., Wisconsin. Leonard H. Simpson IV, delineator, 1991. P&P, HABS, WIS,2-LPOIT.V,1A-.

Completed in 1898, Devils Island Lighthouse, one of the Apostle Islands lighthouses, is an 82-foot-tall steel cylinder. By this time, the cost of steel plate had become affordable enough that it could substitute for cast-iron plate. Originally the lighthouse was supposed to stand without any external support, but the tower shook so much in the wind that a supporting framework was put around it in 1914.

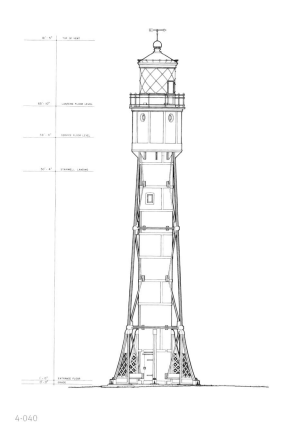

4-040

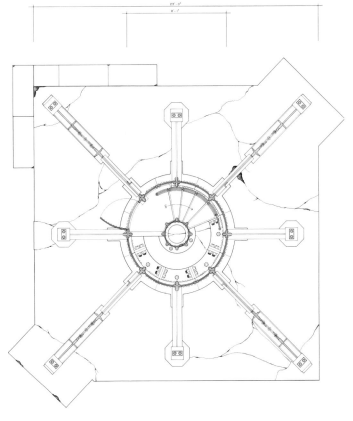

4-041

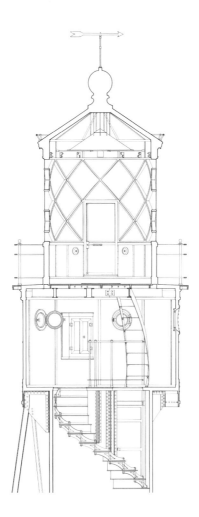

4-042

4-042. Lantern, Devils Island Lighthouse, Lapointe Vic., Wisconsin. Gillian Lewis, delineator, 1991. P&P, HABS, WIS,2-LPOIT.V,1A-.

4-043. East elevation and detail, Devils Island Lighthouse, Lapointe Vic., Wisconsin. Patrick J. Spoden, delineator, 1991. P&P, HABS, WIS,2-LPOIT.V,1B-.

EAST ELEVATION

4-043

REPLACED IN
AUGUST 1991

Pier Lights, Sault Ste. Marie, Michigan

4-044. Pier lighthouse, upper entrance to lock canal, Sault Ste. Marie, Michigan. Between 1890 and 1899. DPCC, LC-D4-11315.

A small, nineteenth-century cast-iron plate lighthouse stood at the upper entrance to the lock canal at Sault Ste. Marie, Michigan.

4-044

4-045. Upper lighthouse at sunset, Sault Ste. Marie, Michigan. Ca. 1908. DPCC, LC-D4-70588.

4-046. Pier lighthouse at the entrance to St. Mary's Canal, Sault Ste. Marie, Michigan. Between 1900 and 1906. DPCC, LC-D4-19191.

4-045

4-046

Ham's Bluff Light, U.S. Virgin Islands

Designed and built by the Danish government in 1915, the lighthouse is on a hill called Ham's Bluff located on the northwestern coast of St. Croix in the U.S. Virgin Islands. It is a cast-iron tower, 35 feet high, on a concrete foundation.

4-047

SKELETON TOWERS

Not long after iron made its debut as a structural material in lighthouses (in the cast-iron plate lighthouses), the first versions of another application of iron to lighthouse construction—skeleton towers—were introduced in the United States.

The skeleton tower was developed to solve a particular problem: how to build a permanent durable structure on compressible soil and water-covered sites. Even though masonry towers stood on some of these sites, their great weight made them liable to settlement. For marine sites, lighthouses had to be built very strong to resist the force of waves and, in northern locations, running ice. Until the introduction of iron pile foundations, marine sites and hazards were usually marked by buoys, unlighted beacons, or lightships.

In skeleton pile construction, metal piles—essentially posts—served as the base for the lighthouse. The base piles were bored or inserted into the ground, and an open framework was built on top. At marine sites, the dwelling and lantern would be built on the framework above the level of high tide. The skeletal foundation did not present a solid mass that the water could work against; waves washed through the legs with little impact on the superstructure or on the ground in which it stood.

Like the cast-iron tower, the origins of the skeleton tower are found in Britain, where the pioneering example, Maplin Sand Lighthouse, was erected on the River Thames and lighted in 1841 (5-001). Maplin Sand Lighthouse had a specific kind of iron pile in its foundation: the screw-pile. As its name suggests, the screw-pile consisted of a very large helicoidal tip on an iron shaft (5-002). The screw-pile improved on ordinary straight piles because the screw head made the pile harder to dislodge and also provided bearing for the superstructure it supported.

American engineers adopted the idea of raising lighthouses above the water on iron pile legs, but they used a variety of pile foundations in addition to screw-piles. These included straight piles set in holes in hard ground or rock, and piles driven into disk footings or sleeves in the ground. The earliest examples of skeleton towers in America, first built in the late 1840s, were all located on marine sites or soft ground. These lighthouses can be classified as either tall towers or small, cottage-style structures. In both cases, the keeper's quarters and storage, in addition to the lantern, were all contained on the structure.

In the 1860s the first skeleton towers were built on land. Like the iron plate towers, this construction type had several advantages: the structures could be prefabricated and therefore readily assembled; they weighed much less than masonry towers; and they could be disassembled and moved. And some lighthouses were indeed moved: for example, Schooner's Ledge Light on the Delaware River—an 1880 tower—was disassembled and brought to Michigan Island in Wisconsin, where it was eventually erected in 1929. For such lighthouses, the keeper's dwelling and other support buildings were separate from the lighthouse tower.

MAPLIN SAND LIGHT-HOUSE.

5-001

5-002

5-001. Maplin Sand Lighthouse, River Thames, England. 1875. Gen. Coll., U.S. Light-House Board, *European light-house systems*, 1875.

5-002. Foundation screw for a screw-pile lighthouse. Ca. 1867. P&P, S, lot 13468.

This image of a screw for a screw-pile gives a sense of the screw's scale. This one measured 5 feet in diameter at the maximum dimension and 1 foot 4 inches at the minimum. In plan the first third of a circumference is a true circle, the rest is an Archimedean spiral. It was made for Jere. P. Smith, Acting Engineer of the Sixth Lighthouse District, by J. Morton Poole & Co., Engineers and Machinists, Wilmington, Delaware, in 1867.

TALL TOWERS WITH DWELLINGS

Because these towers were situated offshore or on sites that were difficult to access, the keepers had to live at the lighthouse. Thus quarters were built in the structure. The tall towers were important lights and usually had to accommodate two or more keepers. When off duty, keepers lived in dwellings on land.

Minot's Ledge Lighthouse, Massachusetts

The first American skeleton lighthouse, Minot's Ledge Lighthouse near Cohasset, Massachusetts, went into operation in January 1850. It was built on Outer Minot's Rock, located over a mile from shore in the midst of breaking waves. The rock's small surface, usually covered with water, was only about 30 feet in diameter, which limited the base dimension of the tower. The skeleton framework consisted of eight outer legs and one central post; these were fixed into holes drilled deep into the rock. They supported a conical iron structure that contained the keeper's room and watch-room and lantern. The structure stood about 70 feet tall.

The conditions to which this lighthouse was exposed were perhaps the harshest in the world at the time. Waves constantly pounded the ledge, causing the structure to vibrate. When the first keeper quit after less than a year on the job because he feared it would overturn, the superintending engineer ordered the lighthouse to be reinforced with additional iron bracing. But in the great storm of April 1851, waves on a swollen tide reached the height of the keeper's room. The sea demolished the lighthouse, killing the two assistant keepers inside. It was replaced with a granite tower (see 2-082–2-087).

IRON LIGHT-HOUSE ON MINOT'S LEDGE.

5-003

5-003. The first lighthouse at Minot's Ledge, near Cohasset, Massachusetts. 1869. Gen. Coll., "Light-Houses," *The Galaxy* (February 1869): 244.

5-004. Destruction of Minot's Ledge Lighthouse, near Cohasset, Massachusetts. LC-USZ62-60355.

5-004

Carysfort Reef Lighthouse, Florida

The first pile tower built off the southern coast of Florida, Carysfort Reef Lighthouse went into operation in 1852. It had eight outside legs and stood 117 feet tall.

5-005

Sand Key Lighthouse, Florida

Completed in 1853, Sand Key Lighthouse was another of the early skeleton towers located off the southern coast of Florida. Although the site was not always under water, it was sandy and sometimes flooded. The structure's unusual form, with seventeen legs in two squares (one inside the other) measuring 50 feet per side on the outside, was an experiment. Engineers worried about the durability of iron in salt water, so the extra legs were added for redundancy. However, it turned out that if it was maintained, iron in water held up well, so this many-legged form was not duplicated.

5-006. Sand Key Lighthouse, off the southern coast of Florida. 1854. LC-USZ62-20076.

5-007. Sand Key Lighthouse, off the southern coast of Florida. J. P. Brooks, photographer, 1967. P&P, HABS, FLA,44-KEY,17-1.

5-006

5-007

5-008

5-009

5-008. Details of the footing, Sand Key
Lighthouse, off the southern coast of
Florida. J. P. Brooks, photographer, 1967.
P&P, HABS, FLA,44-KEY,17-2.

5-009. Details of the connections at the central pile, Sand Key Lighthouse, off the southern coast of Florida. J. P. Brooks, photographer, 1967. P&P, HABS, FLA,44-KEY,17-3.

5-010. Sand Key Lighthouse and weather
bureau station off the southern coast of
Florida. Photocopy of a color postcard.
Unidentified photographer, ca. 1907. P&P,
HABS, FLA,44-KEY,17-5.

5-010

Ship Shoal Lighthouse, Louisiana

Standing on a shoal about 18 miles off the coast of Berwick, Louisiana, in the Mississippi delta, the Ship Shoal Lighthouse replaced a lightship. Placed into service in 1859, this screw-pile lighthouse had eight outer legs arranged in a 40-foot-diameter circle. The tower was about 125 feet tall and had a focal plane of about 117 feet above sea level. The keeper's quarters were inside a circular, two-story metal house from which a cylinder containing a stairway extended to the lantern room. The lighthouse has been repaired and renovated many times over its lifetime. The light was discontinued in 1965.

5-011. Section and elevation, Ship Shoal Lighthouse, Theriot Vic., Louisiana. J. K. Willdin, delineator, 1856. P&P, HAER, LA-12-14.

5-012. View of Ship Shoal Lighthouse from a boat, Theriot Vic., Louisiana. Bill Lebovitch, photographer, 1996. P&P, HAER, LA-12-1.

5-012

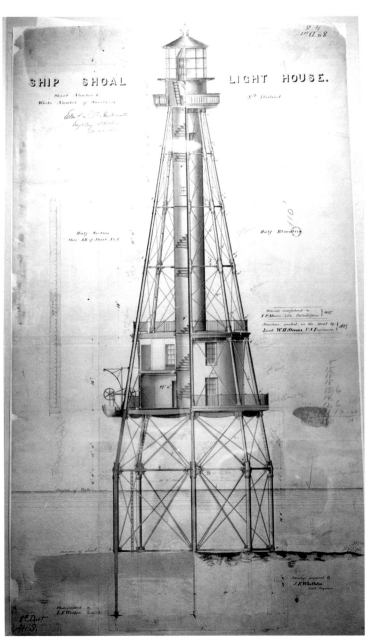

5-011

5-013

5-014

5-013. Ship Shoal Lighthouse, Theriot Vic., Louisiana. Bill Lebovitch, photographer, 1996. P&P, HAER, LA-12-9.

5-014. Keeper's house at Ship Shoal Lighthouse, Theriot Vic., Louisiana. Bill Lebovitch, photographer, 1996. P&P, HAER, LA-12-6.

5-015. Upper part of lighthouse with stairway cylinder, Ship Shoal Lighthouse, Theriot Vic., Louisiana. Bill Lebovitch, photographer, 1996. P&P, HAER, LA-12-4.

5-015

Southwest Pass Lighthouse, Louisiana

Southwest Pass Lighthouse, completed in 1873, was the first iron skeleton to mark one of the ship channels through the Mississippi delta to the Mississippi River. It replaced an earlier masonry tower that the site's compressible soil could not sustain (see 1-072 and 1-073). The foundation consisted of, first, piles driven an average of 32 feet into the soil; then, layers of timber in alternating directions, called grillage, filled with concrete; and a layer of concrete on top. The superstructure was bolted to this platform. The lighthouse had a focal plane of 126 feet. The foundation weighed 900 tons and the superstructure, 293 tons.

5-016. Southwest Pass Lighthouse, vertical section (left half) and elevation (right half), Southwest Pass Entrance, Louisiana. 1874. Gen. Coll., *Annual Report of the Light-House Board*, 1874.

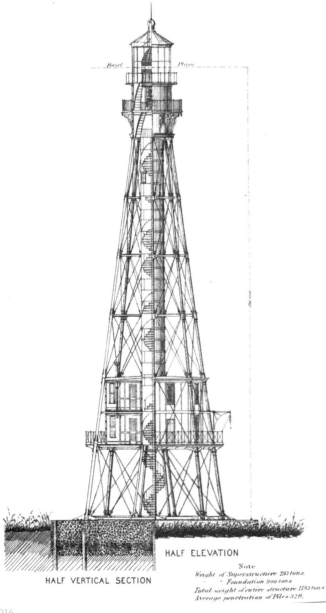

HALF ELEVATION

Note
Weight of Superstructure 293 tons.
" Foundation 900 tons
Total weight of entire structure 1193 tons.
Average penetration of Piles 32 ft.

HALF VERTICAL SECTION

5-016

Trinity Shoal/South Pass Lighthouse, Louisiana

5-017. Trinity Shoal/South Pass Lighthouse, Gulf of Mexico. 1872. Gen. Coll., *Annual Report of the Light-House Board, 1872.*

5-018. Views of the South Pass of the Mississippi including the lighthouse in the upper left, Louisiana. J. O. Davidson, illustrator, 1883. P&P, LC-USZ62-115354.

Although it was designed in 1872 for Trinity Shoal, this tower was not built there but instead was constructed at South Pass, one of the channels through the Mississippi delta. Meanwhile, Trinity Shoal was marked with a lightship. The South Pass tower, also known as Port Ends Lighthouse, later became a rear range light. Lighted in 1881, it stands 105 feet tall.

5-017

5-018

Minor lighthouses built offshore often took the form of houses on stilts. These were usually located nearer to shore than the tall offshore towers.

5-019. Narrows Light, also called Bug Light, near Boston, Massachusetts. 1906. DPCC, LC-D4-19165.

Narrows or Bug Light, Massachusetts

Lighting the way to Boston Harbor and warning of a nearby ledge, the Narrows Lighthouse
stood from 1856 to 1929, when it burned down. It consisted of a wooden house on a
hexagonal frame. It was also called Spit Light because it was situated on Great Brewster
Spit, and Bug Light for its resemblance to an insect with spindly legs hovering over the
water.

5-019

Seven Foot Knoll Lighthouse, Maryland

Seven Foot Knoll Lighthouse, constructed in 1856, was an early example of the sort of cottage-style screw-pile lighthouses that once dotted the Chesapeake Bay. It marked the outer entrance to Baltimore Harbor. The original structure, designed in 1851, had a pyramidal shape, along the lines of the Calcasieu Lighthouse (5-026). The current round, wrought-iron house dates from the late nineteenth century. It has eight outside legs and one central post.

5-020

5-021

5-022

5-023

5-024

5-022. Seven Foot Knoll Lighthouse in the Chesapeake Bay, mouth of the Patapsco River, Maryland. Jay L. Baker, photographer, 1987. P&P, HAER, MD,2-RIVBE.V,1-12.

Detail of the iron "spider" supporting the lighthouse superstructure, platform, and diagonal braces.

5-023. Fog bell at Seven Foot Knoll Lighthouse in the Chesapeake Bay, mouth of the Patapsco River, Maryland. Jay L. Baker, photographer, 1987. P&P, HAER, MD,2-RIVBE.V,1-8.

5-024. Interior of lighthouse, south room on first floor looking west, Seven Foot Knoll Lighthouse in the Chesapeake Bay, mouth of the Patapsco River, Maryland. Jay L. Baker, photographer, 1987. P&P, HAER, MD,2-RIVBE.V,1-18.

Thimble Shoal Lighthouse, Virginia

5-025. Lighthouse at "The Thimble" Shoal, entrance to Hampton Roads, Virginia. 1872. Gen. Coll., *Annual Report of the Light-House Board*, 1872.

This was the first Thimble Shoal Lighthouse, which went into operation in 1872. Located at the entrance to Hampton Roads in Virginia, it replaced a lightship. The structure was a hexagonal wooden cottage on a screw-pile base. It burned in 1880.

5-025

Calcasieu Lighthouse, Louisiana

The Calcasieu Lighthouse went into operation in 1876 at the Calcasieu River near Cameron, Louisiana. It was an iron pyramid on a pile foundation. The form was unusual, but a few others were built on this pattern—its eastern neighbor, the Southwest Reef Lighthouse in Louisiana, and the contemporaneous North Pierhead Light at Erie, Pennsylvania, which also has a square pyramidal form but lacks a pile foundation.

5-026. Calcasieu Lighthouse, near Cameron, Louisiana. 1872. Gen. Coll., *Annual Report of the Light-House Board*, 1872.

5-026

General plan for a screw-pile lighthouse, 1876

5-027. Screw-pile river and harbor lighthouse. 1876. Gen. Coll., *Annual Report of the Light-House Board*, 1876.

Given that military engineers dominated the Light-House Board, it is not surprising that the group sought to produce standard forms for various types of lighthouses. However, standardization did not mean that structures had to be plain and unattractive. This charming and nicely proportioned small lighthouse was a standard plan, prepared while Paul Pelz (see 2-105–2-127) was chief draftsman of the U.S. Light-House Board.

5-027

Mobile Middle Bay Lighthouse, Alabama

The Mobile Middle Bay Lighthouse is a hexagonal wooden house on a hexagonal pile base that stands 54 feet tall. It was lighted in 1885.

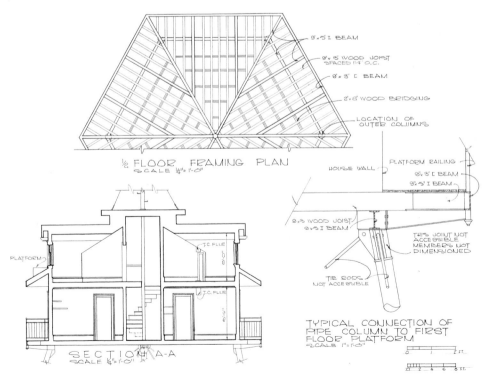

SOUTHWEST ELEVATION
SCALE ⅛"=1'-0'

5-028

½ FLOOR FRAMING PLAN
SCALE ¼"=1'-0"

SECTION A-A
SCALE ¼"=1'-0"

TYPICAL CONNECTION OF
PIPE COLUMN TO FIRST
FLOOR PLATFORM
SCALE 1"=1'-0"

5-029

5-028. Southwest elevation, Mobile Light No. 6639, Mobile Bay, Mobile, Alabama. Michael R. Foil, delineator, 1966. P&P, HABS, ALA,49-MOBI,116-.

5-029. Section and details, Mobile Light No. 6639, Mobile Bay, Mobile, Alabama. James Eley and Carl Rosenberg, delineators, 1966. P&P, HABS, ALA,49-MOBI,116-.

Holland Island Bar Lighthouse, Maryland

This hexagonal wooden lighthouse went into operation in 1889. It stood in the Chesapeake Bay west of Holland Island, at the southern end of the bay. In 1957 the building was hit by missiles fired by U.S. Navy bombers, which apparently overshot a target that was in line with the lighthouse. Two men inside the lighthouse sustained minor injuries.

5-030

Port Mahon Lighthouse, Delaware

Port Mahon Lighthouse, the fourth lighthouse at this location, is a two-story frame house on a screw-pile base. It was lighted in 1903. Compared to other lighthouses of this type, it is architecturally plain and ungainly.

5-031. East side, Port Mahon Lighthouse, the Delaware Bay at the mouth of the Mahon River, Delaware. Kevin R. Bender, photographer, 1982. P&P, HABS, DEL,1-LITCRE.V,1-3.

5-032. Elevations, Port Mahon Lighthouse, the Delaware Bay at the mouth of the Mahon River, Delaware. Raymond Worrall, delineator, 1983. P&P, HABS, DEL,1-LITCRE.V,1-.

5-031

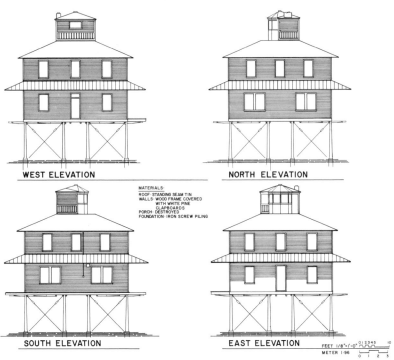

5-032

Unidentified Chesapeake Bay Lighthouse

5-033. Unidentified cottage-style pile light-house probably on the Chesapeake Bay. Theodor Horydczak, photographer, ca. 1920–1950. Theodor Horydczak Collection, LC-H822-T-W04-018.

This is a cottage-style lighthouse like those found on the Chesapeake Bay.

5-033

ONSHORE TOWERS

Unlike their offshore predecessors, onshore towers did not have to include keeper's quarters on the structure. The pile legs supported only a watch-room and lantern. These were usually tall towers. The current *Cape Charles Lighthouse*, in Virginia, is a metal skeleton tower on land that rises 191 feet, making it the tallest skeleton tower in the United States. It became operational in 1895.

5-034. Elevation and entrance detail, LaPointe Lighthouse, near Lapointe, Wisconsin. Krzysztof Koszewski, delineator, 1991. P&P, HABS, WIS, 2-LPOIT.V, 2A-.

LaPointe Lighthouse, Wisconsin

Located south of Madeline Island in Lake Superior, this 60-foot-tall tower has a rectangular cast-iron frame that supports a watch-room and lantern, and a cast-iron cylinder in the center that contains the stairway. It was completed in 1897. The cottage-style lighthouse (a house with a tower) that it replaced was remodeled to serve as the keeper's dwelling.

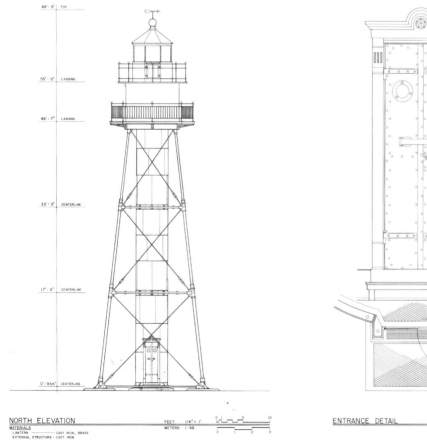

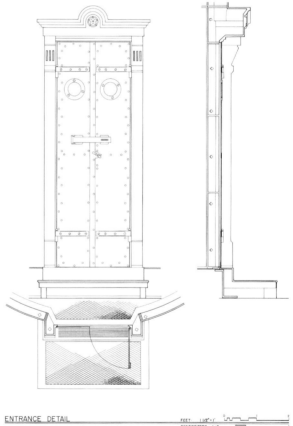

5-034

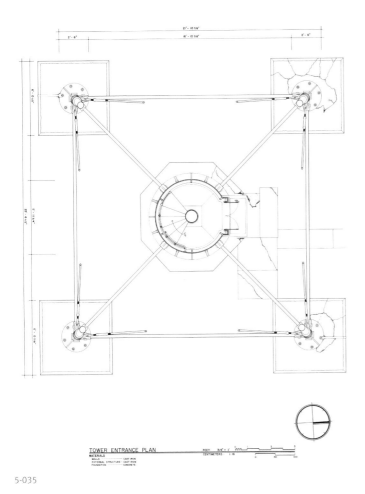

TOWER ENTRANCE PLAN
MATERIALS
WALLS — CAST IRON
EXTERNAL STRUCTURE - CAST IRON
FOUNDATION — CONCRETE

5-035

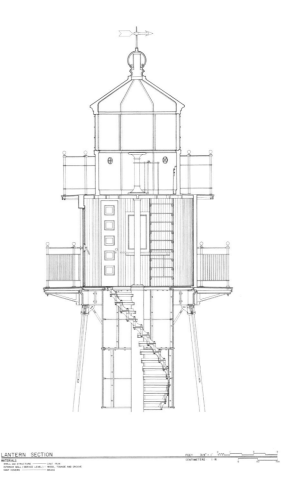

LANTERN SECTION
MATERIALS
SHELL and STRUCTURE — CAST IRON
INTERIOR WALL (SERVICE LEVEL) - WOOD, TONGUE AND GROOVE
VENT COVERS — BRASS

5-036

5-035. Entrance plan, LaPointe Lighthouse, near Lapointe, Wisconsin. Gillian Lewis, delineator, 1991. P&P, HABS, WIS,2-LPOIT.V,2A-.

5-036. Section through lantern, LaPointe Lighthouse, near Lapointe, Wisconsin. Patrick J. Spoden, delineator, 1991. P&P, HABS, WIS,2-LPOIT.V,2A-.

Hillsboro Inlet Light, Florida

Established in 1907, this iron tower stands 137 feet tall.

5-037. Hillsboro Inlet Light, Pompano Beach, Florida. ACME Photo, 1944. P&P, NYWTS, SUBJ/GEOG: LIGHTHOUSES– HILLSBORO INLET–FLORIDA.

5-037

Brazos River Lighthouse, Texas

5-038. Brazos River Lighthouse, Freeport, Texas. P&P, SSF, LIGHTHOUSES—TEXAS, FREEPORT, TEXAS.

Completed in 1896, this square skeleton tower stood about 96 feet tall. The light-station site was sold in 1967 and the new owners destroyed the tower, although the lantern was preserved and is displayed at Brazoria County Historical Museum.

5-038

Reedy Island Rear Range Light, Delaware

This 110-foot tower went into operation in 1910. It was one of the new range lights installed after the main channel in the Delaware River was dredged, which required relocating the existing range lights.

5-039. Reedy Island Range Rear Light, Taylor's Bridge, Delaware. Charles A. Foote and George W. Rineer, photographers, 1976. P&P, HAER, DEL,2-TAYBR,1-1.

5-039

5-040

5-041

5-040. Detail of entry, Reedy Island Range Rear Light, Taylor's Bridge, Delaware. Charles A. Foote and George W. Rineer, photographers, 1976. P&P, HAER, DEL,2-TAYBR,1-4.

5-041. Detail of foundation pier and pile, Reedy Island Range Rear Light, Taylor's Bridge, Delaware. Charles A. Foote and George W. Rineer, 1976. P&P, HAER, DEL,2-TAYBR,1-5.

5-042. Vertical section and plans, Reedy Island Range Rear Light, Taylor's Bridge, Delaware. David Packard, delineator, 1976. P&P, HAER, DEL,2-TAYBR,1-.

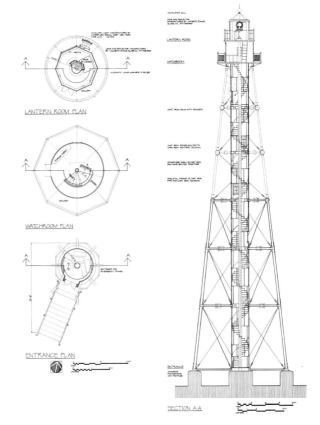

5-042

Coney Island (Norton's Point) Light, New York

By the twentieth century, steel became an affordable alternative to iron for lighthouses. This tower is a steel skeleton standing 70 feet tall; it was lighted in 1920.

5-043

5-044

LIGHTHOUSES ON MARINE FOUNDATIONS

Lighthouses often were needed to mark marine hazards—shoals, reefs, and so on—but building structures on water-covered sites proved challenging. While the pile foundations of iron skeleton lighthouses offered one solution to the problem, it became apparent from an early date that in northern climes these spindly-legged lighthouses were vulnerable to damage from ice. Spring thaws sent ice crashing against their legs and ice built up around them in winter, creating an unwanted mass at water level against which waves and currents could press. One of the first skeleton lighthouses—the Brandywine Shoal screw-pile lighthouse located in the Delaware Bay—was damaged by ice soon after being completed, as were several early pile lighthouses in the Chesapeake Bay. Lightships continued to serve at offshore sites where even skeleton lighthouses could not be economically constructed.

Another solution was to build a solid pier and put a lighthouse on top. These structures had to be strong enough to resist the force of water and ice. Some early piers, or wharfs, were made of timber cribs filled with stones. A more permanent sort of pier could have walls of granite blocks filled between with concrete. The Bergen Point Lighthouse in New Jersey had both kinds of piers: a timber crib, completed in 1849, which deteriorated and was rebuilt a decade later out of granite blocks (6-008). After the Civil War, a simpler means for enclosing a pier was introduced: the iron caisson.

Caissons are essentially watertight boxes used in constructing foundations underwater. They are similar to cofferdams but are distinguished by being self-supporting, whereas cofferdams require surrounding material for their support. Caissons could be open at the top and closed at the bottom (box); open at both ends (open); or, in the case of pneumatic caissons, open at the bottom and closed at the top and supplied with compressed air. All these types were used to build lighthouse foundations. Pneumatic caissons were made famous by John and Washington Roebling, who used them to build the foundations for the towers of the Brooklyn Bridge. In that project, compressed air kept the caissons dry so workmen could excavate the river bottom from inside them. As the workers removed ground under the caisson, the bridge towers were constructed on top; this weight pressed the caisson down until it eventually settled on a firm level. Iron or steel plate were the usual materials for building caissons. They were fabricated on land, floated to a prepared site, and lowered in place. Then the inside was excavated and the structure settled into the ground, either through gravity or loads placed on the top of the caisson, or by other means. Filled with concrete, the caisson served as a platform for the lighthouse.

The pioneering project that applied caisson technology to lighthouse foundations was the repair of Waugoshance Lighthouse by William Sooy Smith, a civil engineer and U.S. Military Academy graduate. This lighthouse, a conical brick tower, was erected in 1851 on Waugoshance Shoal, an exposed reef about 2 1/2 miles from shore in Lake Michigan, at the western entrance to the Straits of Mackinac. Its original foundation consisted of a timber crib filled with stones. In 1867–1870, to make a more secure base for the lighthouse, Smith rebuilt the foundation by sinking a caisson and building courses of stone on top. Abandoned in 1912, this lighthouse still survives, although in deteriorated condition. The earliest example of a lighthouse with an iron tubular foundation was the Duxbury Pier Light, put into service in 1871. Pneumatic caissons were used to build the foundations of a few lighthouses—for example, Fourteen Foot Bank Light in Delaware (1888) and Sabine Bank Light in Louisiana (1906). More commonly, caissons used in lighthouse foundations were the box or open types.

Any sort of lighthouse could be built on a pier foundation. A common form for light-houses on the iron caisson foundations was the iron-plate type, which extended the iron plating of the foundation up through the superstructure. These usually had projecting, covered galleries above the foundation caisson, and the resulting shape resembled a sparkplug. While most of the sparkplug-shaped lighthouses had iron-plate towers, Spring Point Ledge Light in Maine had a brick tower (1897; 6-038–6-043). Moreover, iron super-structures did not have to be plain. Examples of ornate iron lighthouses on caissons are Ship John Shoal Lighthouse in the Delaware Bay (1877) and its twin at Southwest Ledge, Connecticut (1877; 6-020–6-021).

Later in the nineteenth century, caisson lighthouses began to replace earlier skeleton lighthouses. For example, the historic skeleton lighthouse at Brandywine Shoal in the Delaware Bay was replaced with a caisson lighthouse in 1914. Like the offshore skeleton lighthouses, the pier and caisson lighthouses contained quarters for the keepers.

Maine Lighthouses on Granite Piers

Although situated close to land, several lighthouses in Maine were built on granite piers, specifically the lights at Marshall Point (1857), Ram Island (1883), Doubling Point (1899), Isle Au Haut (1907), and Whitlock's Mill (1910). Doubling Point is a wooden octagon; all the others are cylindrical brick structures on granite piers. Except for Whitlock's Mill, all are or were connected by bridges to the mainland.

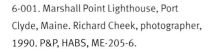

6-001. Marshall Point Lighthouse, Port Clyde, Maine. Richard Cheek, photographer, 1990. P&P, HABS, ME-205-6.

6-001

6-002

6-003

6-004

6-002. Ram Island Lighthouse, Ram Island, Boothbay Harbor, Maine. Richard Cheek, photographer, 1990. P&P, HABS, ME-206-3.

6-003. Doubling Point Lighthouse, Arrowsic, Maine. Richard Cheek, photographer, 1989. P&P, HABS, ME-188-1.

6-004. Doubling Point Lighthouse showing pier, Arrowsic, Maine. Richard Cheek, photographer, 1989. P&P, HABS, ME-188-2.

6-005

6-006

6-005. Interior, Doubling Point Lighthouse, Arrowsic, Maine. Richard Cheek, photographer, 1989. P&P, HABS, ME-188-3.

6-006. Isle Au Haut Lighthouse, Robinson Point, Maine. Richard Cheek, photographer, 1991. P&P, HABS, ME-212-4.

6-007. Whitlock's Mill Lighthouse, St. Croix River, near Calais, Maine. Richard Cheek, photographer, 1992. P&P, HABS, ME-209-2.

6-007

Bergen Point Lighthouse, New Jersey

Built during the period 1857–1859 at the junction of Newark Bay and Kill Van Kull, the lighthouse stood on a 60-foot-diameter granite pier. It was discontinued in 1949 and torn down.

6-008. Bergen Point Lighthouse, Newark Bay, New Jersey. 1874. Gen. Coll., *Harper's New Monthly Magazine* 48 (March 1874): 466.

6-008

Craighill's Channel Front Beacon, Maryland

6-009. Front beacon, Craighill's Channel Range or Leading Lights, Chesapeake Bay, near Baltimore, Maryland. American Photo-Relief Printing Co., 1873. Gen. Coll., *Annual Report of the Light-House Board*, 1873.

An early example of the cast-iron caisson with a cast-iron plate tower is the Front Beacon of Craighill's Channel Range Lights (lighted in 1873, but not fully finished until 1875), located in the Chesapeake Bay at the entrance to Baltimore Harbor. A base for the tubular foundation was made of piles. To steady the tube during construction, a grillage was built around the bottom; this held it in place until it could be loaded and sunk to position and then filled with concrete.

6-009

Penfield Reef Lighthouse, Connecticut

Located on a shoal southeast of Fairfield Beach, near the entrance to Bridgeport Harbor in Long Island Sound, the lighthouse is on a cylindrical granite pier standing in 5 feet of water. It went into operation in 1874.

The pier is faced with nine courses of granite, tapering from 48 feet 9 inches at the bottom to 46 feet 6 inches at the top, and filled with concrete. Riprap surrounds the bottom to protect it from erosion. Like others of this type, the pier had a hollow section in the center that served as a cellar and cistern.

The lighthouse is a cottage type—a square stone dwelling, 28 feet per side, with a wooden mansard roof and an integral tower that rises 35 feet. This plan, a square dwelling with an octagonal tower, was common in lighthouses of the period, notably those on the Hudson River.

6-010

The lighthouse's pier was built by F. Hopkinson Smith (1838–1915), a contracting engineer, artist, and writer. Smith began erecting marine structures in the 1860s, and his projects included ice-breakers, breakwaters, and jetties. He also worked on challenging offshore lighthouses similar to Penfield Reef, such as Race Rock Lighthouse on Fishers Island in Long Island Sound (1870–78) and Butlers Flat Lighthouse near New Bedford, Massachusetts (1898). He built the foundation for the pedestal on which the Statue of Liberty stands (see AP-011). In his spare time, Smith painted and drew, and he exhibited his artwork. He began to write later in life and eventually published many stories and novels. Some of these drew on his experiences as a marine engineer, for example, *Caleb West, master diver.*

6-010. Penfield Reef Lighthouse, Long Island Sound, Connecticut. 1874. Gen. Coll., *Annual Report of the Light-House Board,* 1874.

opposite
6-011. Penfield Reef Lighthouse, looking northeast, Long Island Sound, Connecticut. Robert Brewster, Warren Jagger Photography, Inc., photographer, 1997. P&P, HAER, CONN, 1-BRIGPO,9-3.

6-012. Detail of south elevation, Penfield Reef Lighthouse, Long Island Sound, Connecticut. Robert Brewster, Warren Jagger Photography, Inc., photographer, 1997. P&P, HAER, CONN, 1-BRIGPO,9-5.

6-013. Lantern, Penfield Reef Lighthouse, Long Island Sound, Connecticut. Robert Brewster, Warren Jagger Photography, Inc., photographer, 1997. P&P, HAER, CONN, 1-BRIGPO,9-7.

6-014. Interior, second floor stairway with rope rail, Penfield Reef Lighthouse, Long Island Sound, Connecticut. Robert Brewster, Warren Jagger Photography, Inc., photographer, 1997. P&P, HAER, CONN, 1-BRIGPO,9-11.

6-011

6-012

6-013

6-014

Hudson-Athens Lighthouse, New York

The 1874 Hudson-Athens Lighthouse sits on an irregularly shaped granite pier in the Hudson River. The lighthouse is made of brick with stone trim.

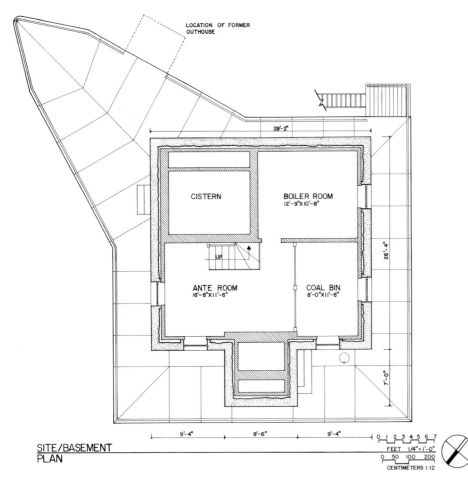

LOCATION OF FORMER OUTHOUSE

CISTERN

BOILER ROOM
12'-9"X10'-8"

ANTE ROOM
16'-8"X11'-6"

COAL BIN
8'-0"X11'-6"

UP

28'-2"

26'-4"

7'-0"

9'-4"   9'-6"   9'-4"

SITE/BASEMENT
PLAN

FEET 1/4"=1'-0"
0 1 2 3 4 5 6 7
0 50 100 200
CENTIMETERS 1:12

6-015

6-015. Site and basement plan, Hudson-Athens Lighthouse, Athens, New York. Steven M. Morrotta, delineator, 1987. P&P, HABS, NY,20-ATH,2-, sheet no. 2.

opposite
6-016. Southwest elevation, Hudson-Athens Lighthouse, Athens, New York. Steven M. Morrotta, delineator, 1987. P&P, HABS, NY,20-ATH,2-, sheet no. 4.

6-017. Northeast elevation, Hudson-Athens Lighthouse, Athens, New York. Steven M. Morrotta, delineator, 1987. P&P, HABS, NY,20-ATH,2-, sheet no. 5.

6-018. Plans of Hudson-Athens Lighthouse, Athens, New York. Steven M. Morrotta, delineator, 1987. P&P, HABS, NY,20-ATH,2-, sheet no. 3.

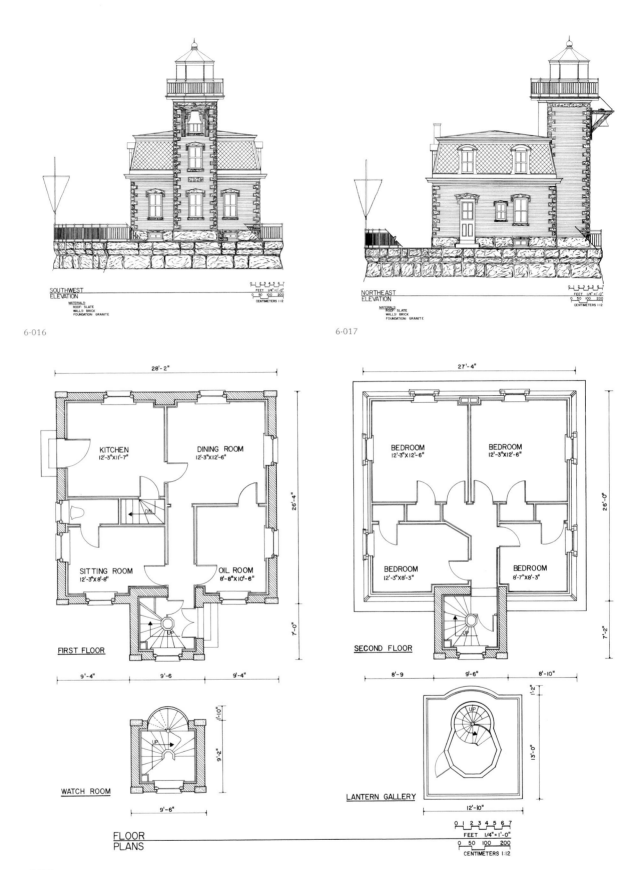

SOUTHWEST
ELEVATION

MATERIALS:
ROOF: SLATE
WALLS: BRICK
FOUNDATION: GRANITE

FEET 1/4"=1'-0"
0 50 100 200
CENTIMETERS 1:12

6-016

NORTHEAST
ELEVATION

MATERIALS:
ROOF: SLATE
WALLS: BRICK
FOUNDATION: GRANITE

FEET 1/4"=1'-0"
0 50 100 200
CENTIMETERS 1:12

6-017

28'-2"

KITCHEN
12'-3"X11'-7"

DINING ROOM
12'-3"X12'-6"

26'-4"

SITTING ROOM
12'-3"X8'-8"

OIL ROOM
8'-8"X10'-6"

7'-0"

FIRST FLOOR

9'-4"   9'-6"   9'-4"

27'-4"

BEDROOM
12'-3"X12'-6"

BEDROOM
12'-3"X12'-6"

26'-0"

BEDROOM
12'-3"X8'-3"

BEDROOM
8'-7"X8'-3"

7'-2"

SECOND FLOOR

8'-9   9'-6"   8'-10"

1'-10"

9'-2"

WATCH ROOM

9'-6"

1'-2"

13'-0"

LANTERN GALLERY

12'-10"

FLOOR
PLANS

0 1 2 3 4 5 6 7
FEET 1/4"=1'-0"
0 50 100 200
CENTIMETERS 1:12

6-018

Stepping Stones Lighthouse, New York

Like the Penfield Reef Lighthouse (6-010–6-014), Stepping Stones Light sits on a granite pier in Long Island Sound. The house and tower are brick; the tower stands 38 feet tall. It became operational in 1877.

6-019. Stepping Stones Lighthouse, near Kings Point, New York. Al Ravenna, photographer, 1958. P&P, NYWTS, SUBJ/GEOG: LIGHTHOUSES–STEPPING STONES LIGHTHOUSE.

6-019

Southwest Ledge (New Haven Breakwater) Light, Connecticut

6-020. Elevation and vertical section, Southwest Ledge Light, Long Island Sound, Connecticut. 1894. Gen. Coll., *Annual Report of the Light-House Board*, 1894.

6-021. Exhibit of aids to navigation presented by the U.S. Light-House Board at the 1876 Centennial Exposition, Philadelphia, Pennsylvania. 1876. P&P, LC-USZ62-57609.

Two architecturally ornate lighthouses on cast-iron, tubular foundations demonstrated that iron plate was not inevitably boilerplate. Ship John Shoal Lighthouse in the Delaware Bay, New Jersey, and its twin, Southwest Ledge (New Haven Breakwater) Light in Long Island Sound near the entrance to New Haven Harbor, Connecticut, were completed in 1877.

Southwest Ledge Lighthouse had been fabricated, but not yet erected, at the time of the Centennial Exposition in Philadelphia in 1876, and it became a feature in the Light-House Board's exhibit there (see also IN-061).

6-021

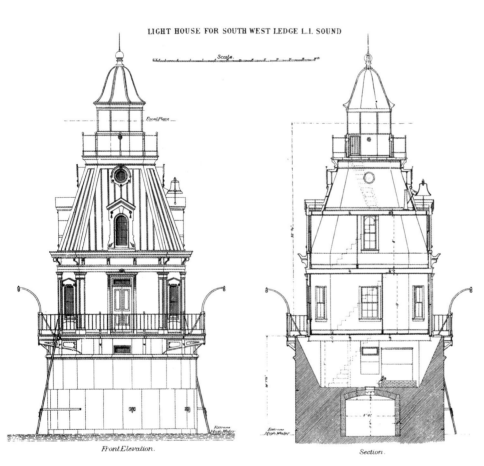

LIGHT HOUSE FOR SOUTH WEST LEDGE L.I. SOUND

Front Elevation.

Section.

6-020

Port Austin Reef Light, Michigan

This structure sits atop an 80-foot-diameter, octagonal pier on a shoal in Lake Huron. The 60-foot-tall, square brick tower, measuring 16 feet per side, was lighted in 1878. The pier was modified in 1899 and rebuilt in 1937, with 5 feet of concrete added to the sides. Within the tower were three bedrooms and a kitchen. The attached structure is a fog signal building.

6-022. Port Austin Reef Light, Lake Huron, Michigan. Between 1900 and 1906. DPCC, LC-D4-12353.

6-023. Port Austin Reef Light, Lake Huron, Michigan. Between 1895 and 1910. DPCC, LC-D4-32162.

6-022

6-023

Stannard's Rock Lighthouse, Michigan

Stannard's Rock Lighthouse, lighted in 1882, is an example of a traditional-looking lighthouse on a tubular foundation. Set on a shoal in Lake Superior, its foundation pier was modeled on that of Spectacle Reef Lighthouse (see 2-090–2-091). Like all offshore towers, this was a complicated project that took six years to complete. The lighthouse is a conical stone tower that stood about 100 feet above the lake. In this case, the foundation tube was made of wrought iron rather than cast iron; it measured 62 feet in diameter at the top, and 28 to 30 feet deep. The surface was paved with Belgian blocks.

To build the foundation, a square timber crib with an octagonal opening in the center was built onshore, filled with stones, and then towed to the site, where it was put in position and sunk. The sides were raised with the addition of more timber and the space filled with more stones, and then the structure was decked over. This served as a protection pier, which held the tubular foundation in place during construction. The permanent foundation, an iron tube, was fabricated and then towed over and lowered into the opening. After it settled on the uneven, rocky reef, the cylinder was made watertight, pumped out, completed to its full height, and filled with concrete. The workmen lived at the site, on a ship or in barracks built on the temporary crib structure. In image 6-024 the square crib is still in place, but this was removed in 1883.

6-024

STANNARDS ROCK LIGHT HOUSE.
LAKE SUPERIOR. *Plate 13.*

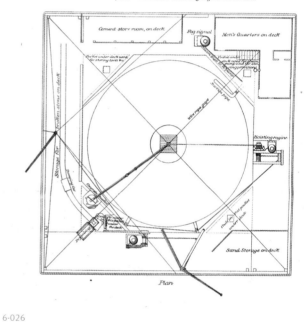

Section of piers and elevations of hoisting engine and derricks.

Plan

6-026

6-025

6-027

6-025. Method of drilling range posts and ringbolts, Stannard's Rock Lighthouse, in Lake Superior, Marquette Vic., Michigan. 1882. Gen. Coll., *Annual Report of the Light-House Board*, 1882.

This illustration, from a report on the construction, shows workmen marking the location of the temporary crib.

6-026. Section of piers and elevation of the hoisting engine and derricks (top) and plan of work platform for constructing the lighthouse, Stannard's Rock Lighthouse, in Lake Superior, Marquette Vic., Michigan. 1882. Gen. Coll., *Annual Report of the Light-House Board*, 1882.

6-027. Stannard's Rock Lighthouse from a Coast Guard boat coming to rescue men after an explosion in the lighthouse, in Lake Superior, Marquette Vic., Michigan. UPI Telephoto, 1961. P&P, NYWTS, SUBJ/GEOG: LIGHTHOUSES–STANNARD ROCK LIGHT-HOUSE–LAKE SUPERIOR.

Tarrytown (Kingsland Point) Light, New York

6-028. Tarrytown Lighthouse, Hudson River south of Kingsland, New York. Between 1900 and 1920. DPCC, LC-D4-73009.

Completed in 1883, Tarrytown Lighthouse is a cast-iron caisson with a conical cast-iron plate tower.

6-028

6-029

6-030

6-029. Tarrytown Lighthouse, Hudson River south of Kingsland, New York. U.S. Coast Guard Photo, 1956. P&P, NYWTS, SUBJ/GEOG: LIGHTHOUSES–TARRYTOWN LIGHT–TARRYTOWN, NEW YORK–HUDSON RIVER.

Close-up of the lighthouse in the summer, at the time (1956) the home of keeper Richard Moreland and his family.

6-030. Tarrytown Lighthouse, Hudson River south of Kingsland, New York. International News Photo, 1934. P&P, NYWTS, SUBJ/GEOG: LIGHTHOUSES–TARRYTOWN LIGHT–TARRYTOWN, NEW YORK–HUDSON RIVER.

View of the lighthouse on a February day when the river was frozen so solid that visitors could walk out to the lighthouse.

Robbins Reef Light, New York

6-031. Robbins Reef Lighthouse, Upper New York Bay, New York. Dick DeMarsico, photographer, 1945. NYWTS, SUBJ/GEOG: LIGHTHOUSES—ROBBINS REEF—NEW YORK BAY.

6-032. Interior, Robbins Reef Lighthouse, Upper New York Bay, New York. Dick DeMarsico, photographer, 1945. NYWTS, SUBJ/GEOG: LIGHTHOUSES—ROBBINS REEF—NEW YORK BAY.

This photograph shows the small living area of the lighthouse, where the staff ate and spent their time when not on duty or sleeping. Ralph Rexinger and Joaquim H. Brito are at the table, and Olaf Andersen is standing by the stove. After meals, the table would be moved away to make a sitting room.

Similar to Tarrytown Light and also completed in 1883, Robbins Reef Light is in Upper New York Bay, off the northern end of Staten Island. It is a 45-foot-tall cast-iron tower lined with brick on a granite block platform.

6-031

6-032

Delaware Breakwater Light, Delaware

This light was placed in the entrance to the Delaware Bay in the vicinity of the Brandywine Shoal pile lighthouse, which had been plagued by ice. Lighted in 1885, it has a cast-iron caisson foundation and a conical cast-iron plate tower.

6-033. Delaware Breakwater Lighthouse, Lewes Harbor, Delaware. Ca. 1891. LC-USZ62-92460.

6-033

Detroit River Lighthouse, Michigan

6-034. Detroit River Lighthouse, Bar Point Shoal, Lake Erie, Michigan. 1885. Gen. Coll., *Annual Report of the Light-House Board*, 1885.

The Detroit River Lighthouse (established in 1885) was built at the western end of Lake Erie near the mouth of the Detroit River on a site covered with about 22 feet of water. The foundation pier consisted of a timber crib—a watertight box with a watertight floor—made in a hexagonal shape with the pointed ends serving as ice-breakers. This structure was towed to the site, sunk, and filled with concrete; then a wall of stone blocks backed with concrete was constructed on top of it, to a height of 11 feet above the lake surface. The top of the pier was covered with stone pavers. Finally, the bottom of the pier was surrounded with riprap to protect it from erosion. The structures built on the pier consisted of a 32-foot-tall, cast-iron plate lighthouse with a brick lining, containing four stories, a watchroom, and a lantern; and a separate wooden fog-signal house.

6-034

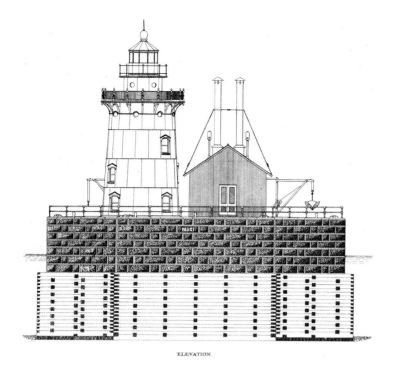

6-035

ELEVATION

6-035. Elevation, Detroit River Lighthouse, Bar Point Shoal, Lake Erie, Michigan. 1885. Gen. Coll., *Annual Report of the Light-House Board*, 1885.

6-036. Section, Detroit River Lighthouse, Bar Point Shoal, Lake Erie, Michigan. 1885. Gen. Coll., *Annual Report of the Light-House Board*, 1885.

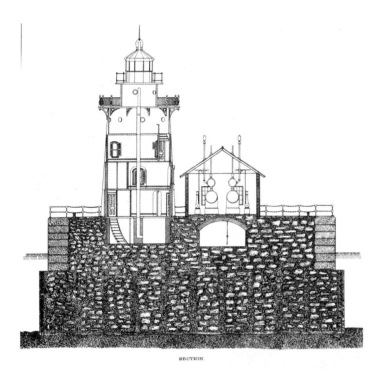

6-036

SECTION.

Deer Island Light, Massachusetts

6-037. Deer Island Lighthouse, Boston, Massachusetts. Ca. 1906. DPCC, LC-D4-18918.

Located in the water off Deer Island, on the northern side of the channel to Boston Harbor, Deer Island Lighthouse was established in 1890. Its foundation pier consisted of a cast-iron cylinder; this was built within a temporary platform that was removed after completion. The pier measured about 30 feet high, 33 feet in diameter at the base, and 37 feet 9 inches across its flared top. The first 19 feet of the base was filled while the rest was lined with brick, creating a cellar that housed an engine-room, toilet, and storerooms. The superstructure was also made of iron in a slightly conical shape and lined with brick. It had three stories, a covered verandah at the first level, and a gallery at the level of the watch-room. The height of its focal plane was about 63 feet above the water. It is no longer extant.

6-037

Spring Point Ledge Light, Maine

Standing on a dangerous obstruction along the main channel into Portland Harbor, Spring Point Ledge Light has an iron caisson foundation. Unlike most other sparkplug-shaped lighthouses, its cylindrical superstructure is made of brick rather than cast iron. It went into service in 1897. The lighthouse was connected to the mainland in 1950–51 by a granite breakwater.

6-038. Spring Point Ledge Lighthouse, Portland Harbor, Maine. Ca. 1905. P&P, LC-USZ62-115970.

6-039. Spring Point Ledge Lighthouse, Portland Harbor, Maine. Ca. 1906. DPCC, LC-D4-18927.

opposite
6-040. Interior doorway and stairs to third floor, Spring Point Ledge Lighthouse, Portland Harbor, Maine. Richard Cheek, photographer, 1989. P&P, HABS, ME, 3-PORTS, 3-7.

6-041. Lens in lantern room, Spring Point Ledge Lighthouse, Portland Harbor, Maine. Richard Cheek, photographer, 1989. P&P, HABS, ME, 3-PORTS, 3-8.

6-042. View from northeast of Spring Point Ledge Lighthouse, Portland Harbor, Maine. Richard Cheek, photographer, 1989. P&P, HABS, ME, 3-PORTS, 3-3.

6-043. Interior of second floor, Spring Point Ledge Lighthouse, Portland Harbor, Maine. Richard Cheek, photographer, 1989. P&P, HABS, ME, 3-PORTS, 3-6.

6-038

6-039

6-040

6-041

6-042

6-043

Rockland Harbor Breakwater Lighthouse, Maine

In the late nineteenth century, a long, granite breakwater was built from Jameson Point into Rockland Harbor on West Penobscot Bay. A lighthouse was constructed at the end of the breakwater in 1902 on a timber and granite pier. The superstructure consisted of a brick tower and sound signal building attached to a frame dwelling that was one and a half stories tall.

6-044. Rockland Harbor Breakwater Lighthouse, Rockland, Maine. Richard Cheek, 1991. P&P, HABS, ME-7-ROCLA, 6-2.

6-044

Romer Shoal Lighthouse, New York

6-045. Romer Shoal Lighthouse, Lower New York Bay, New York. Al Ravenna, photographer, 1967. NYWTS, SUBJ/GEOG: LIGHT-HOUSES–ROMER SHOAL LIGHT.

Located in lower New York Bay, Romer Shoal Light (established in 1898) resembled Robbin's Reef Light (6-031 and 6-032), except that its base was a concrete caisson surrounded with riprap instead of a granite block pier. Its daymarking was the opposite of Robbin's Reef: a light-colored bottom and dark-colored top.

6-045

Mile Rocks Lighthouse, California

Marking some rocks in the entrance to the Golden Gate, Mile Rocks Lighthouse had a high foundation made of steel plates and concrete. The lighthouse itself was made of steel plates. It was completed in 1904 and served until 1966, when the tower was removed.

6-046. Mile Rocks Lighthouse, San Francisco, California. 1924. P&P, LC-USZ62-59210.

6-046

Peck Ledge Light, Connecticut

6-047. Peck Ledge Lighthouse, Long Island Sound near Norwalk, Connecticut. G. S. North, photographer, ca. 1906. P&P, LC-USZ62-127106.

6-048. Peck Ledge Lighthouse, Long Island Sound near Norwalk, Connecticut. G. S. North, photographer, ca. 1906. P&P, LC-USZ62-127105.

Completed in 1906, Peck Ledge Light is formed of a cast-iron and concrete caisson foundation with a conical cast-iron plate tower on top.

6-047

6-048

Baltimore Lighthouse, Maryland

The Baltimore Lighthouse stands in the south entrance to Craighill Channel in the Chesapeake Bay. First lighted in 1908, it is a sturdy brick octagon on a timber and cast-iron caisson foundation. The tower is two and a half stories and stands 38 feet tall.

In 1964 the fuel in this lighthouse was converted to nuclear power, making this the first lighthouse in which this fuel source was tested. The Coast Guard thought nuclear power could be used to operate lighthouses in remote places. In the picture, a 4,600-pound isotopic fuel cell generator is being installed in the lighthouse. The Atomic Energy Commission (forerunner to the Nuclear Regulatory Commission) developed the 60-watt generator at a time when nuclear power seemed a likely option for many power needs. The generator was used for a year, after which it was removed and the nuclear-powered lighthouse program was abandoned owing to safety issues.

6-049. A nuclear power generator being installed in the Baltimore Lighthouse, Chesapeake Bay, Maryland. U.S. Coast Guard, photographer, 1964. P&P, SSF, LIGHTHOUSES—MARYLAND—1964.

6-049

Rock of Ages Light, Michigan

6-050. South elevation, Rock of Ages Lighthouse, Copper Harbor Vic., Michigan. Bryan L. Cooper, delineator, 1995. P&P, HABS, MICH,42-COPHAR.V,3-.

6-051. Southeast elevation, Rock of Ages Lighthouse, Copper Harbor Vic., Michigan. Mark G. Ostojich, delineator, 1995. P&P, HABS, MICH,42-COPHAR.V,3-.

This tower, one of the tallest and brightest in the Great Lakes, stood on the hazardous Rock of Ages reef off the western end of Isle Royale in Lake Superior. Its base is a cylindrical platform. After the rock was blasted to level it, a steel cylinder, 50 feet in diameter and 25 feet high, was placed on the rock and filled with concrete. Although the lighthouse built on this base has a classic appearance, it is actually a steel skeleton enclosed in brick. Completed in 1908, the tower stands about 117 feet above the water level.

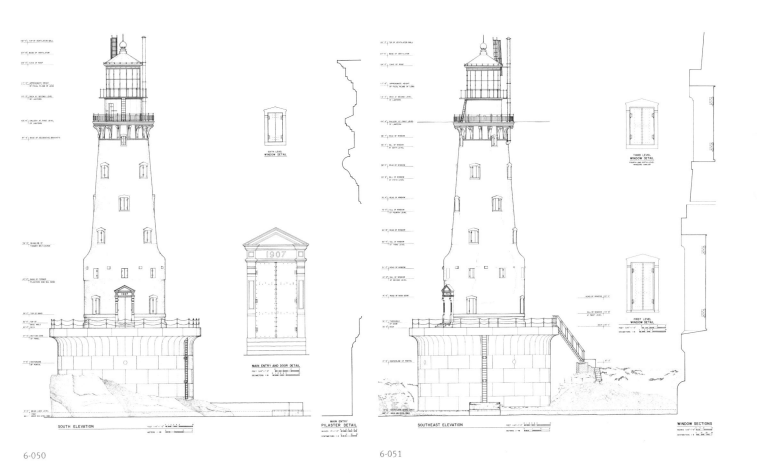

6-050

6-051

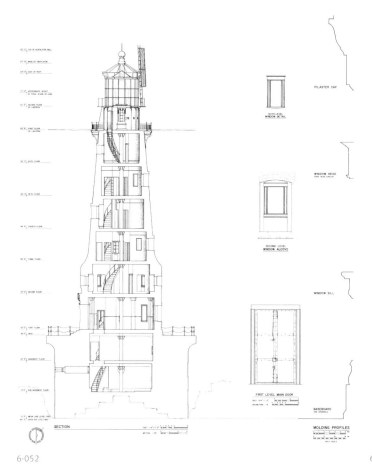

6-052

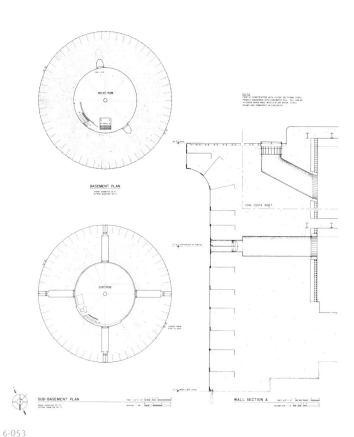

6-053

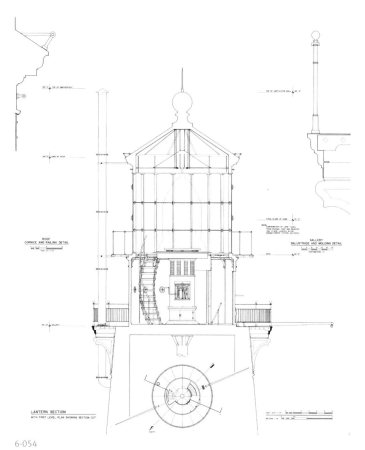

6-054

6-052. Section, Rock of Ages Lighthouse, Copper Harbor Vic., Michigan. Michael J. Kolonauski, delineator, 1995. P&P, HABS, MICH,42-COPHAR.V,3-.

6-053. Basement and subbasement plans, and section through the caisson, Rock of Ages Lighthouse, Copper Harbor Vic., Michigan. Mark G. Ostojich, delineator, 1995. P&P, HABS, MICH,42-COPHAR.V,3-.

6-054. Section through the lantern, Rock of Ages Lighthouse, Copper Harbor Vic., Michigan. Marc F. Gee, James Ferguson, and Mary Ellen Strain, delineators, 1995. P&P, HABS, MICH,42-COPHAR.V,3-.

New London Ledge Lighthouse, Connecticut

6-055. New London Ledge Lighthouse, looking east, New London, Connecticut. Robert Brewster, Warren Jagger Photography, Inc., photographer, 1997. P&P, HAER, CONN, 6-NEWLO,16-2.

Lighted in 1909, New London Ledge Lighthouse is cottage style, although in this case "mansion style" would seem a more appropriate description. The lantern rises from the center of a handsome brick dwelling with granite trim and a mansard roof. Moreover, despite its traditional appearance, the lighthouse was framed in brick and concrete in order to make it noncombustible. It is located on a dangerous ledge at the eastern side of the entrance to Connecticut's New London Harbor, at the eastern end of Long Island Sound. It sits on a square concrete pier, 50 feet per side, with a crib foundation protected at the base with riprap. The original protecting crib was removed in 1938 and replaced with a steel enclosure.

6-055

6-056

6-057

6-056. Basement of New London Ledge Lighthouse showing in the center the hollow tube for the clockwork mechanism weights, New London, Connecticut. Robert Brewster, Warren Jagger Photography, Inc., photographer, 1997. P&P, HAER, CONN, 6-NEWLO,16-6.

6-057. Third floor recreation room, New London Ledge Lighthouse, New London, Connecticut. Robert Brewster, Warren Jagger Photography, Inc., photographer, 1997. P&P, HAER, CONN,6-NEWLO,16-9.

6-058. Lantern and watch-room, New London Ledge Lighthouse, New London, Connecticut. Robert Brewster, Warren Jagger Photography, Inc., photographer, 1997. P&P, HAER, CONN, 6-NEWLO,16-11.

6-058

Angel's Gate/Los Angeles Harbor Lighthouse, California

6-059. Angel's Gate/Los Angeles Harbor Lighthouse, San Pedro, California. Wittemann Collection, P&P, SSF, LIGHTHOUSES—CALIF., SAN PEDRO.

Situated at the end of a 9,000+-foot-long breakwater in San Pedro, Angel's Gate Lighthouse marks the entrance to the harbor of Los Angeles, California. Standing 69 feet tall, the cylindrical structure consists of a steel frame enclosed in concrete and steel plates. Its foundation is a 40-foot concrete square base surrounded with rocks. It was established in 1913 and since then has withstood very rough seas. With its distinctive paint pattern—black vertical stripes between white panels—it also serves as a daymark.

6-059

TWENTIETH- CENTURY MATERIALS

The beginning of the twentieth century was a time of tremendous innovation in building materials and engineering. During the 1890s, the first skeleton frame buildings went up in the United States; these were made of metal frames enclosed with thin walls. The frames supported the floor, roof, and other loads, while the enclosing walls, called curtain walls, served to keep out the weather. One great advantage of skeleton frame construction compared with load-bearing, masonry construction was that large structures could be erected much faster. Since the frame cannot be seen, lighthouses with brick curtain walls look like traditional masonry structures.

Another new material was reinforced concrete. In the nineteenth century, lighthouse engineers had used concrete to make massive structures such as foundations. But in the twentieth century, techniques for building superstructures (the above-ground parts of a building) out of concrete were applied to lighthouses. Concrete was reinforced with steel to gain tensile strength. The first reinforced concrete tower in the United States was the Point Arena Lighthouse in Mendocino County, California, which went into service in 1908. It replaced an earlier lighthouse that was destroyed in the great San Francisco earthquake of 1906. Engineers found that reinforced concrete buildings withstood the earthquake better than other kinds of construction.

Skeleton towers, now made of steel rather than iron, continued to be built on land and offshore. A new type of offshore skeleton tower was the Texas Tower, so called because it resembles the offshore platforms used by oil drillers along the Texas coast. Texas Towers were introduced to replace lightships, which continued to mark a number of sites in the 1950s. Although the Texas Towers hardly look like lighthouses, they could be considered updated versions of the skeleton lighthouses. The first Texas Tower was put into operation in Buzzard's Bay, off the Massachusetts coast, in 1961 (7-017). Only six towers of this type were constructed.

STEEL FRAME

7-001. Split Rock Lighthouse under construction, Two Harbors Vic., Minnesota. L. D. Campbell, photographer, 1909–1910. L. D. Campbell, Minnesota Historical Society, negative number 44317.

7-002. View looking south with fog signal buildings in the foreground, Split Rock Lighthouse, Two Harbors Vic., Minnesota. Jet Lowe, photographer, 1990. P&P, HAER, MINN,38-TWOHA.V,1-3.

Steel did not see widespread use in building frames until the 1890s—especially after the 1893 depression, when prices for steel structural members fell.

Split Rock Lighthouse, Minnesota

The Split Rock Lighthouse, built 1910 on the northern shore of Lake Superior in the vicinity of Two Harbors, Minnesota, has a metal frame and brick and concrete curtain walls. Yet the octagonal "brick" lighthouse that resulted has a traditional, and very picturesque, appearance.

7-001

7-002

Round Island Passage Lighthouse, Michigan

Located in the Straits of Mackinac between Lakes Huron and Michigan, the Round Island Passage Lighthouse was built in 1948. It was made of reinforced concrete topped with a metal tower. It was designed to be unattended, hence the narrow tower.

7-003. Round Island Passage Lighthouse, Straits of Mackinac, Michigan. U.S. Coast Guard, 1949. P&P, SSF, LIGHTHOUSES—MICHIGAN—1949, ROUND ISLAND PASSAGE LIGHT.

7-003

Charleston Lighthouse, South Carolina

7-004. Charleston Lighthouse, Charleston, South Carolina. U.S. Coast Guard, 1962. P&P, SSF, LIGHTHOUSES—MICHIGAN— 1949, ROUND ISLAND PASSAGE LIGHT.

Lighted in 1962, the structure stands on Sullivan's Island, on the northern side of the entrance to Charleston Harbor. When it went into service, it was the most powerful lighthouse in the Western Hemisphere. It has a triangular profile, is made of steel with aluminum alloy cladding, and stands 140 feet tall. In addition to its other outstanding features, it was the first American lighthouse to have an elevator. It is also one of the last lighthouses constructed in the United States.

7-004

REINFORCED CONCRETE

Although some reinforced concrete buildings had been erected in the late nineteenth century, the material did not see widespread use until the first decade of the twentieth century.

Scotch Cap Light, Alaska

Located near the western end of Unimak Island, this light marked the Unimak Pass, the main passage through the Aleutian Islands into the Bering Sea. This modern and sturdy-looking tower went into service in 1940. But in 1946 an enormous tidal wave set off by two earthquakes swept the building away, killing the five men stationed at the lighthouse.

7-005. Scotch Cap Lighthouse, Unimak, Aleutian Islands, Alaska. ACME Photo, 1946. P&P, NYWTS, SUBJ/GEOG: LIGHT-HOUSES—SCOTCH CAP—UNIMAK, ALEUTIAN ISLANDS.

7-005

Molokai (Kalaupapa) Lighthouse, Hawaii

7-006. View of Molokai (Kalaupapa) Lighthouse from the west-northwest, Kalaupapa Peninsula, Hawaii. Jack E. Boucher, photographer, 1991. P&P, HABS, HI,3-KALA.V,5-A-3.

After Hawaii's aids to navigation became the responsibility of the Light-House Board in 1904, the Board and its successor, the Bureau of Lighthouses, evaluated the islands' coast to determine where lights needed to be improved and new lights introduced. The Molokai Lighthouse, built in 1909, was a new coastal light. The concrete tower, with nearly vertical walls, stands 138 feet tall.

7-006

7-007

7-008

7-007. Molokai (Kalaupapa) Lighthouse, Kalaupapa Peninsula, Hawaii. Jack E. Boucher, photographer, 1991. P&P, HABS, HI,3-KALA.V,5-A-4.

7-008. Base of Molokai (Kalaupapa) Lighthouse, Kalaupapa Peninsula, Hawaii. Jack E. Boucher, photographer, 1991. P&P, HABS, HI,3-KALA.V,5-E-2.

7-009. Residence No. 1 at Molokai (Kalaupapa) Lighthouse, Kalaupapa Peninsula, Hawaii. Jack E. Boucher, photographer, 1991. P&P, HABS, HI,3-KALA.V,5-B-2.

7-009

Diamond Head Lighthouse, Hawaii

7-010. Diamond Head Lighthouse, Diamond Head/Oahu Island, Hawaii. Between 1930 and ca. 1940. P&P, LC-USZ62-66984.

A lighthouse at this location, built in 1899, predated the Light-House Board's entry in Hawaii. The original tower was replaced in 1918 by a concrete structure that stands 57 feet tall.

7-010

Anacapa Island Lighthouse, California

Standing on Anacapa Island, one of the Channel Islands in Santa Barbara Channel off Port Hueneme, this lighthouse is a concrete cylinder that stands 39 feet tall. It became operational in 1932.

7-011. Anacapa Island Lighthouse, Anacapa Island, near Port Hueneme, California. 1972. P&P, HABS, CA-2335-B.

7-011

Barbers Point Lighthouse, Hawaii

7-012. Barbers Point Lighthouse, Kalaeloa/Oahu Island, Hawaii. Pan Pacific Press, between 1933 and ca. 1940. P&P, LC-USZ62-66983.

Barbers Point Lighthouse, on Oahu Island, was lighted in 1933. It is a 71-foot-tall concrete tower.

7-012

Tree Point Light, Alaska

Lighted in 1935, Tree Point Light has a square tower that stands 66 feet high. It has Art Deco–style details.

7-013. Tree Point Lighthouse, Revillagigedo Channel, Alaska. U.S. Coast Guard, 1946. P&P, NYWTS, SUBJ/GEOG: LIGHTHOUSES–TREE POINT LIGHT–ALASKA.

7-013

Oak Island Lighthouse, North Carolina

7-014. Oak Island Lighthouse, near the mouth of Cape Fear River, North Carolina. 1958. P&P, NYWTS, SUBJ/GEOG: LIGHT-HOUSES—NORTH CAROLINA.

The Oak Island Lighthouse, built in 1958, is a concrete cylinder that stands 169 feet tall. The walls are only 8 inches thick from top to bottom of the tower. The paint for its day-marking—three bands in different colors—was mixed with the concrete, so the tower never needs to be repainted.

7-014

MODERN SKELETON TOWERS

The skeleton tower evolved so that in the twentieth century it was made of steel rather than cast and wrought-iron. Around 1923, the Lighthouse Service had developed standard plans for steel skeleton towers and iron pipe towers. Both types had square bases, and the sizes of their structural members were proportioned to allow for expected corrosion.

Copper Harbor Light, Michigan

This 60-foot-tall steel skeleton tower was built in 1933. The legs of the lighthouse were fixed to concrete piers. The (new) Copper Harbor Light replaced an 1866 cottage-style lighthouse, which still stands a little to the east of the new tower (see 3-019).

7-015. Copper Harbor Light, Copper Harbor Vic., Michigan. James C. Massey, photographer, 1995. P&P, HAER, MICH,42-COPHAR.V,4-2.

7-016. Footing, Copper Harbor Light, Copper Harbor Vic., Michigan. James C. Massey, photographer, 1995. P&P, HAER, MICH,42-COPHAR.V,4-5.

7-015

7-016

Buzzard's Bay Entrance Light, Massachusetts

Like the skeleton pile lighthouses of a century earlier, Texas Tower light stations stood on pile legs. However, they were larger and could be built in much deeper water. Buzzard's Bay Entrance Light (established in 1961) had a helicopter platform and facilities for oceanographic and meteorological equipment. But its advanced facilities were found unnecessary, and it has been replaced with a smaller structure.

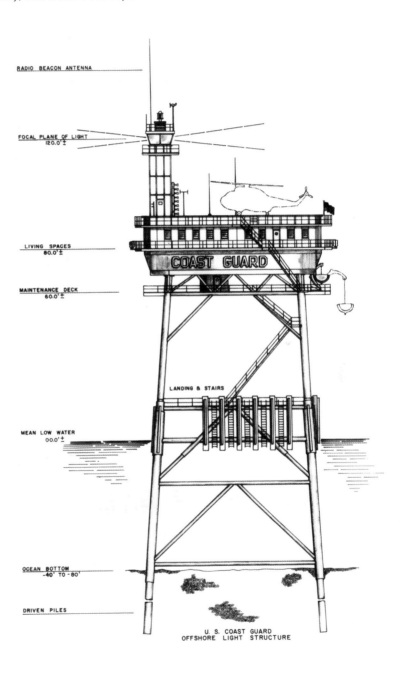

7-017

LIGHTHOUSES IN ART

Lighthouses are popular subjects for artists and photographers. Many of the images used to illustrate lighthouse construction in this book are works of art. Those included here, in the Appendix, are more subjective. Usually lighthouses are represented realistically, even if dramatically. To many contemporary artists they may seem too sentimental as subject matter, but more abstract representations of lighthouses do exist. Naturally, most images of lighthouses show them in the daytime, when the artists can see them, rather than in the dark of night, when the structures are actually working. Lighthouses are wonderful structures, whether simple and traditional or technologically advanced and made of the high-tech materials of their day. They will undoubtedly endure as subjects beloved by artists and the public, as long as they survive.

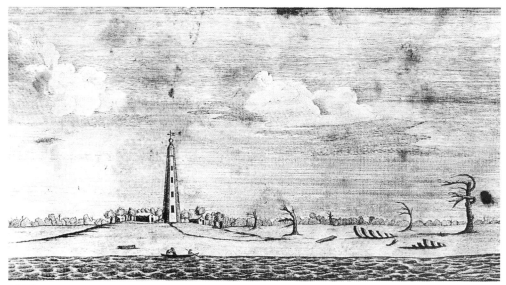

AP-001

AP-002

AP-003

AP-001. View of the lighthouse on Cape Henlopen, Delaware, taken at sea. August 1780. Gen. Coll., *The Columbian magazine, or, Monthly miscellany* (February 1788), LC-USZ62-31786.

Even in colonial times, artists drew views of lighthouses, such as this one of Cape Henlopen Lighthouse.

AP-002. Montauk Point Lighthouse, Long Island, New York. 1871. Gen. Coll., *Harper's New Monthly Magazine* 43 (September 1871): 481.

AP-003. Montauk Point Lighthouse seen from on the water, Long Island, New York. P&P, LC-USZ62-50716.

Lighthouses, as well as travelogues that recounted visits to remote lighthouses, were popular subjects for nineteenth-century magazine readers, and these stories were illustrated with drawings that featured lighthouses.

AP-004. Owl's Head Lighthouse, Rockland Harbor, Maine. Obpacher Brothers. P&P, LC-USZ62-39504.

Maine has many picturesque lighthouses, which have inspired generations of artists.

AP-005. *The Lighthouse — Maine* Coast. Edward Hopper, 1919–1923. P&P, LC-USZ62-43195.

New England lighthouses were a favorite subject for Edward Hopper.

AP-006. Dice Head Lighthouse, Castine, Maine. Ca. 1893. P&P, Souvenir View Books, Maine.

This was drawn at a time when the stone lighthouse was clad so that it looked like a hexagonal wooden tower.

AP-004

AP-005

AP-006

AP-007

AP-007. Minot's Ledge Light in a gale, near Cohasset, Massachusetts. 1869. Gen. Coll., *The Galaxy 7* (February 1869): 244b.

AP-008. Matinicus Rock Lighthouse, Matinicus Rock, Maine. W. Taber, artist, 1897. Gen. Coll., *The Century* 54 (June 1897): 222.

The drama of sea-rock and island lighthouses being pounded by waves in stormy weather is a popular theme.

AP-009. Night image of Cape Cod Light, also called Highland Light, near Truro, Massachusetts. Cosmas V. Cosmades, photographer, ca. 1967. P&P, LC-USZ62-74414.

Usually, lighthouses are portrayed in the daylight, but their main reason for being is to light up the night.

AP-008

AP-009

AP-010. Lighthouse and skyline, Chicago, Illinois. 1930. P&P, LC-USZ62-126290.

Lighthouse artists usually prefer subjects in rural settings, but harbor lighthouses are the oldest type. This photograph sets its subject against the Chicago skyline.

AP-011. The Great Bartholdi Statue, *Liberty Enlightening the World*. Currier & Ives, ca. 1885. LC-USZ62-20515

The Statue of Liberty, originally known as *Liberty Enlightening the World*, served as a lighthouse following its dedication in 1886.

AP-012. Cape May Point Lighthouse, Cape May Point, New Jersey. Jack E. Boucher, photographer, 1977. P&P, HABS, NJ,5-CAPMAP, 2-1.

Although Historic American Building Survey (HABS) documentation is intended to objectively record information about the nation's historic structures, HABS photographers sometimes cannot resist artful compositions, such this one in which the subject is framed by the ruins of its predecessor.

AP-010

AP-012

AP-011

AP-013

AP-014

AP-013. Lighthouse, woodcut. John Bernhardt, 1953. FP-XX-B498, no. 3 (D size).

Most artists represent lighthouses realistically. Here is a less common abstract composition with a lighthouse.

AP-014. Lighthouse, Palmer Park, Detroit, Michigan. Between 1890 and 1901. DPCC, LC-D4-7393.

Three-dimensional replicas of lighthouses are as popular as two-dimensional representations. This replica decorated the shores of a lake in Palmer Park, Detroit, Michigan.

BIBLIOGRAPHY

An important source of information on individual lighthouses was the Historic American Building Survey (HABS) and the Historic American Engineering Record (HAER) collection, which is housed in the Prints and Photographs department of the Library of Congress. A program of the National Park Service, HABS/HAER produces graphic (photographs, measured drawings) and written documentation of historically significant architectural, engineering, and industrial sites and structures. Some of these sites and structures no longer exist.

Lighthouse websites constituted another useful source of information. The number of these websites is extraordinary. Some deal with lighthouses overall, others focus on lighthouses in particular regions. Many lighthouses have their own websites. Often websites repeat information (including inaccurate information) from others. The websites I found most useful and reliable include:

Lighthouse Heritage, Maritime Heritage Program, National Park Service
www.cr.nps.gov/maritime/lt_index.htm
(updates the publication *Inventory of Historic Light Stations*, 1994)

New England Lighthouses: A Virtual Guide, created by Jeremy D'Entremont
www.lighthouse.cc

Seeing the Light, Lighthouses of the Western Great Lakes, researched and written by
    Terry Pepper
www.terrypepper.com/lights/index.htm

Lighthousefriends.com
www.lighthousefriends.com

Chesapeake Chapter of the U.S. Lighthouse Society
www.cheslights.org/heritage.htm

National Park Service websites for lighthouses within parks, such as the Apostle Islands
National Lakeshore website

www.nps.gov/apis

For the early history of lighthouses, I used reports to Congress and by congressional committees dealing with lighthouses, which can be found in the Congressional Serial Set. From 1852 to 1910, the *Annual Reports of the Light-House Board* provide information on all aspects of the U.S. lighthouse service.

Abbot, Edward. "Light-Houses." *The Galaxy* 7, no. 2 (February 1869): 237–48.

Barnard, John G. "Lighthouse Construction." In *Johnson's New Illustrated Universal Cyclopedia.* New York: A. J. Johnson & Son, 1877.

———. "Lighthouse Engineering as Displayed at the Centennial Exhibition." *Transactions of the American Society of Civil Engineers* 8 (1879): 55–82.

Black, William M. *The United States Public Works.* New York: John Wiley & Sons, 1895.

Blunt, Edmund. *The American Coast Pilot*, 11th ed. New York: Edmund & George Blunt, 1827.

Candage, R. G. F. "Boston Light and the Brewsters." *New England Magazine* 13, no. 2 (October 1895): 131–47.

Cullum, George W. *Biographical Register of the Officers . . . of the United States Military Academy at West Point, N.Y.,* 3rd ed. Boston: Houghton, Mifflin, 1891.

Dean, Love. *Lighthouses of the Florida Keys.* Sarasota: Pineapple Press, 1998.

Elliot, George H. *Report of a Tour of Inspection of European Light-House Establishments, Made in 1873.* Washington, DC: G.P.O., 1874; also Exec. Doc. 54, 43:1.

Gieseler, E. A. "The Illumination of Maritime Coasts." *Manufacturer and Builder* 19, no. 2 (February 1887): 40–42; 19, no. 3 (March 1887): 62; 19, no. 4 (April 1887): 82–83.

Gonzalez, Henry. "Screw-Pile Lighthouses, Part II: Growth and Demise." *Chesapeake Channel Marker* 10 (Winter 1998): 1–8.

Guelzo, Carl. "Failure on Minot's Ledge." *Tradition* 2 (January 1959): 51–58.

Harrison, Tim, and Ray Jones. *Lost Lighthouses.* Guilford, CT: Globe Pequot Press, 2000.

Holland, Francis Ross, Jr. *America's Lighthouses: Their Illustrated History since 1716.* Brattleboro, VT: Stephen Greene Press, 1972.

———. *Lighthouses.* New York: MetroBooks, 1995.

Johnson, Arnold. *The Modern Light-House Service.* Washington, DC: GPO, 1889.

Jones, Ray. *Lighthouse Encyclopedia.* Guildford, CT: Globe Pequot Press, 2004.

Kobbe, Gustav. "Heroism in the Lighthouse Service." *The Century: A Popular Quarterly* 54, no. 2 (June 1897): 219–31.

———. "Life in a Lighthouse (Minot's Ledge)." *The Century: A Popular Quarterly* 47, no. 3 (January 1894): 364–75.

Lawrence, Charles A. "The Building of Minot's Ledge Lighthouse." *New England Magazine* 15, no. 2 (October 1896): 131–45.

Lewis, I. W. P. "Screw Piles." *Appleton's Mechanics' Magazine and Engineers' Journal* 2 (December 1852): 268–70.

"Light-House Construction and Illumination." *Putnam's Monthly Magazine* 8, no. 44 (August 1856): 198–213.

Nordhoff, Charles. "The Light-Houses of the United States." *Harper's New Monthly Magazine* 48, no. 286 (March 1874): 465–77.

"Our Light-House Establishment." *Putnam's Monthly Magazine* 7, no. 42 (June 1856): 544–658.

Parsons, Charles. "Montauk Point, Long Island." *Harper's New Monthly Magazine* 43, no. 256 (September 1871): 481–94.

Putnam, George. *Lighthouses and Lightships of the United States.* Boston: Houghton Mifflin, 1917.

———. *Sentinel of the Coasts: The Log of a Lighthouse Engineer.* New York: W. W. Norton, 1937.

Rhein, Michael J. *Anatomy of the Lighthouse.* New York: Barnes & Noble Books, 2000.

Snow, Edward R., updated by Jeremy D'Entremont. *The Lighthouses of New England.* Beverly, MA: Commonwealth Editions, 2002.

———. *The Story of Minot's Light.* Boston: Yankee Publishing, 1940.

Stevenson, Alan. *A Rudimentary Treatise on the History, Construction and Illumination of Lighthouses.* London: John Weale, 1850.

Stevenson, Robert. *An Account of the Bell Rock Light-House.* Edinburgh: A. Constable et al., 1824.

Stevenson, Thomas. *Lighthouse Construction and Illumination*. London: E. & F. Spon, 1881.

Updike, Richard. "Winslow Lewis and the Lighthouses." *American Neptune* 28 (1968): 31–48.

U.S. Department of Commerce. *The United States Lighthouse Service, 1915*. Washington, DC: GPO, 1916.

U.S. Department of the Interior. *Inventory of Historic Light Stations*. Washington, DC: National Park Service History Division, 1994.

U.S. Light-House Board. *Report of the Officers Constituting the Light-House Board . . . to Inquire into the Condition of the Light-House Establishment of the United States . . .* (February 1852). Senate Exec. Doc. 28, 32:1.

U.S. Lighthouse Establishment. *Compilation of Public Documents and Extracts from Reports and Papers Relating to Light-Houses . . . 1789 to 1871*. Washington, DC: G.P.O., 1871.

Vojtech, Pat. *Lighting the Bay: Tales of Chesapeake Lighthouses*. Centerville, MD.: Tidewater Publishers, 1996.

Weiss, George. *The Lighthouse Service: Its History, Activities and Organization*. Baltimore, MD: Johns Hopkins Press, 1926.

Wermiel, Sara. *Army Engineers' Contributions to the Development of Iron Construction in the Nineteenth Century*, Essays in Public Works History no. 21. Kansas City, MO: Public Works Historical Society, 2002.

GLOSSARY

BEACON. An aid to navigation projecting from and attached to the earth's surface. It can be lighted or unlighted. Lighthouses are a kind of lighted beacon. Unlighted beacons are also called *daymarks* or *day-beacons*.

CAISSON. A large, watertight container, usually cylindrical, used for building platforms on water-covered or water-saturated sites. Caissons could be open at the top and closed at the bottom (box); open at both ends (open); or, in the case of pneumatic caissons, open at the bottom and closed at the top and supplied with compressed air. A caisson is made on land, towed to its site, lowered in place, and then excavated from within or settled by gravity, depending on the type. Filled with concrete, it made a base for a lighthouse.

CATOPTRIC. Reflecting, as in the case of the reflecting lights that were the standard type in the United States before the 1850s.

CHARACTER. The appearance of the light from a lighthouse. The character of lights within a region is varied so that a mariner can identify each lighthouse correctly and determine his location. Characters include fixed, flashing, revolving, grouped (generally paired), and colored lights.

COFFERDAM. A temporary dam that excludes water from a site normally covered with water where construction is planned.

CRIB. A structure formed of several layers of beams, each layer perpendicular to the one below, which served as a part of a building's foundation. For lighthouse foundations, these were usually made of timber, then sunk in water and filled with stones or concrete to keep them in place. This was an old method of construction, long used to make the foundations of wharfs and *piers*; cribs also could be used as temporary retaining forms around *caisson* or masonry foundations. As long as water covered them, the wooden forms endured.

DAY-BEACON. See *daymark*.

DAYMARK. A *beacon* visible during the day that helps a mariner determine his location. Unlighted beacons are daymarks. Lighthouses are often painted with bright colors or patterns so that they can serve as daymarks.

DEACTIVATED. Removed from service.

DIOPTRIC. Refracting, as in the *Fresnel lens*, which bends light to a chosen direction.

ESTABLISH. To place an authorized aid to navigation in operation for the first time.

FIXED LIGHT. A steady, non-flashing beam.

FOCAL PLANE. The height of the center of a beam of light above the surrounding water.

FOG SIGNAL. A device that makes a loud noise, used to signal the locations of lighthouses during storms or fog when the lights are obscured. Cannons, bells, whistles, horns, and sirens have served as fog signals.

FRESNEL LENS. A system of convex lenses and prisms that *refract* light to create a concentrated, horizontal beam. Named for its inventor, civil engineer and mathematician Augustin Jean Fresnel, the lenses came in several forms and sizes, which were known as *orders*.

FUEL. The material that is burned in a lamp to produce light. Early lighthouse fuels included wood, coal, wax (candles), whale oil, and kerosene. Modern fuels include electricity and solar power; an attempt to use nuclear power to fuel lighthouse lamps was discontinued.

GRILLAGE. Same as *crib*.

KEEPER. The person responsible for maintaining the *light station* and attending the light source and other aids to navigation at the station, including *fog signals*. Keepers usually lived by or in the lighthouse.

LAMP. The source of light in a lighthouse.

LANTERN. The glassed-in housing on top of a lighthouse that contains the *lamp* and *lens*.

LEDGE. A large rock formation that sticks up from the surrounding ground.

LENS. An optical system made of prismatic and curved glass used to concentrate or magnify a *lamp*'s light.

LIGHTHOUSE. A structure that supports a light that can be seen from a distance.

LIGHT-HOUSE BOARD. A nine-member board, dominated by the military, that Congress established in 1852 to manage and build aids to navigation throughout the United States. Its duties were transferred to a new Bureau of Lighthouses in the Department of Commerce and Labor in 1910.

LIGHT STATION. The complex of buildings and facilities that supports a lighthouse. In addition to the light tower, a light station usually includes a *keeper*'s dwelling and may also contain an *oil house*, sound signal building, cistern, boathouse, workshop, and other structures.

LIGHTSHIP. A moored vessel displaying a light that acts as a lighthouse. These were placed at locations, usually near hazards, where it would be too expensive if not impossible to build a lighthouse.

OIL HOUSE. A small building where *fuel* for the lighthouse *lamps* was stored.

ORDERS. The classes of *Fresnel lens*, based on size and number of *lamps*. First order lights were the largest and brightest, and could be seen from the greatest distance; sixth order lights were the smallest.

PIER. (1) A manmade structure built in navigable waters for use as a landing place or to protect or form a harbor. (2) A mass of masonry that acts as a support, such as a granite and concrete platform under an offshore lighthouse.

PILE. A post of wood or iron driven into the ground that forms the foundation of a structure. Wooden piles were used in series when a construction site had compressible ground or was covered with water. Iron piles were used as legs for skeleton lighthouses. A *screw-pile* had a large screw at its end and could be forced down by turning it.

RANGE. The distance at sea from which a light can be seen.

RANGE LIGHTS. Lights in pairs, a lower one at the water and a taller one inland, which when lined up vertically let a mariner know his position relative to the channel. An inner (or rear) range light is the light that is situated behind the other as viewed from the water. The outer (or front) range light is the light that is situated in front of the other as viewed from the water.

REFLECTOR. In a lighthouse light apparatus, a mirror or shiny metal surface that throws back light to the direction where it is wanted.

REFRACT. To bend rays of light.

RIP RAP. Rocks and stones piled up around a structure to help stem erosion.

SCREW-PILE. A metal post with a spiraling tip, like a screw, that is drilled into soft ground.

SHOAL. A shallow area, such as a sandbar or rock formation.

TOWER. The structure supporting the *lantern* room of a lighthouse

VENTILATOR. The perforated ball in the center of the roof of many *lanterns* that exhausts heat from the *lamps*.

WATCH-ROOM. A room, usually located beneath the *lantern* room, outfitted with windows through which a lighthouse *keeper* could observe water conditions.

INDEX

Locators that include a section designator followed by a hyphen (e.g., IN-010, 2-153, 3-090) refer to numbered captions. All other locators are page numbers. Individuals who created the original images used in this collection, or the structures depicted, are identified as follows: arch. = architect; art. = artist; bldr. = builder; del. = delineator; eng. = engraver; engr = engineer; ph. = photographer; ill. = illustrator

ABOUT THE CD-ROM

The CD-ROM includes direct links to four of the most useful online catalogs and sites, which you may choose to consult in locating and downloading images included on it or related items. Searching directions, help, and search examples (by text or keywords, titles, authors or creators, subject or location, and catalog and reproduction numbers, etc.) are provided online, in addition to information on rights and restrictions, how to order reproductions, and how to consult the materials in person.

1. The Prints & Photographs Online Catalog (PPOC) (http://www.loc.gov/rr/print/catalogabt.html) contains over one million catalog records and digital images representing a rich cross-section of graphic documents held by the Prints & Photographs Division and other units of the Library. It includes a majority of the images on this CD-ROM and many related images, such as those in the HABS and HAER collections cited below. At this writing the catalog provides access through group or item records to about 50 percent of the Division's holdings.

SCOPE OF THE PRINTS AND PHOTOGRAPHS ONLINE CATALOG

Although the catalog is added to on a regular basis, it is not a complete listing of the holdings of the Prints & Photographs Division, and does not include all the items on this CD-ROM. It also overlaps with some other Library of Congress search systems. Some of the records in the PPOC are also found in the LC Online Catalog, mentioned below, but the P&P Online Catalog includes additional records, direct display of digital images, and links to rights, ordering, and background information about the collections represented in the catalog. In many cases, only "thumbnail" images (GIF images) will display to those searching outside the Library of Congress because of potential rights considerations, while onsite searchers have access to larger JPEG and TIFF images as well. There are no digital images for some collections, such as the Look Magazine Photograph Collection. In some collections, only a portion of the images have been digitized so far. For further information about the scope of the Prints & Photographs online catalog and how to use it, consult the Prints & Photographs Online Catalog *HELP* document.

For further information about how to search for Prints & Photographs Division holdings not represented in the online catalog or in the lists of selected images, submit an email using the "Ask a Librarian" link on the Prints & Photographs Reading Room home page or contact: Prints & Photographs Reading Room, Library of Congress, 101 Independence Ave., SE, Washington, D.C. 20540-4730 (telephone: 202-707-6394).

2. The American Memory site (http://memory.loc.gov), a gateway to rich primary source materials relating to the history and culture of the United States. The site offers more than seven million digital items from more than 100 historical collections.

3. The Library of Congress Online Catalog (http://catalog.loc.gov/) contains approximately 13.6 million records representing books, serials, computer files, manuscripts, cartographic materials, music, sound recordings, and visual materials. It is especially useful for finding items identified as being from the Manuscript Division and the Geography and Map Division of the Library of Congress.

4. Built in America: Historic American Buildings Survey/Historic American Engineering Record, 1933–Present (http://memory.loc.gov/ammem/collections/habs_haer) describes and links to the catalog of the Historic American Buildings Survey (HABS) and the Historic American Engineering Record (HAER), among the most heavily represented collections on the CD-ROM.